Microsoft Networking
Made Simple

Microsoft Networking Made Simple

P.K.McBride

MADE SIMPLE
BOOKS

Made Simple
An imprint of Butterworth-Heinemann
Linacre House, Jordan Hill, Oxford OX2 8DP
A division of Reed Educational and Professional Publishing Ltd

ℛ A member of the Reed Elsevier plc group

OXFORD   BOSTON   JOHANNESBURG
MELBOURNE   NEW DELHI   SINGAPORE

First published 1996

© P.K.McBride, 1996

TRADEMARKS/REGISTERED TRADEMARKS
Computer hardware and software brand names mentioned in this book are protected
by their respective trademarks and are acknowledged.

British Library Cataloguing in Publication Data
A catalogue record for this book is available from the British Library

ISBN 0 7506 2837 5

Typeset by P.K.McBride, Southampton

Archtype, Bash Casual, Cotswold and Gravity fonts from Advanced Graphics Ltd
Icons designed by Sarah Ward © 1994
Printed and bound in Great Britain by Scotprint, Musselburgh, Scotland

Contents

Preface

Nowadays you can use Microsoft products to handle all aspects of networking from passing files between a couple of PCs in a small office, to communicating with the rest of the wired world.

This book is intended mainly for those people who work on a local area network in an office – or at home – or who want to have e-mail and other access to the Internet. It will show you how to set up a small office network, but the emphasis is on using the facilities rather than technical details of installation and maintenance.

The first 40 pages is purely about work within a local area network. The rest is about e-mail and other forms of communications both within the office and beyond to the rest of the world.

You must have a suitable (V32 or V34) fax/modem to handle your external communications. Apart from that, the only special equipment that you need right now is Windows 95 and a computer capable of running it. Other essential or useful software can be obtained from the Internet – and most of it is free!

If you want to know more about Windows 95 or the Internet, try the companion books in this series:

"*Windows 95 Made Simple*" , "*The Internet Made Simple*" and "*Internet Resources Made Simple*".

1 Windows 95 networks

Networks

A network is a set of computers joined together by cables or radio links. Thus joined they can communicate with each other, share data and have access to each other's printers or other peripherals. The size and nature of networks vary enormously. Key variations are:

- The number and type of attached computers. These may be all PCs or Apples (or other computers), or a mixture of desktop computers and larger machines.

- The nature of the connections between them. The link may be through a cable which runs directly from one to another, or indirectly through modems and the telephone system.

- The degree to which the network's users can share its resources. All users may have full access to all data and peripherals on the network, or there may be different categories of users, which varying levels of access.

We can usefully divide networks into three broad types:

- Local Area Network (LAN)
- Wide Area Network (WAN)
- Internetwork

In this book we will be looking at aspects of all three types of networks, using Windows 95, Microsoft Network and Microsoft applications.

Take note

There are three levels to any kind of network. At the bottom are the hardware and software to control the communications between the linked computers. At the top are the applications that work across the network. In between is the software that enables you to access the network's facilities.

Windows 95 networking

- ❑ You can use Windows 95 with two different styles of LANs – peer-to-peer and server networks.

- ❑ A *peer-to-peer* network consists only of PCs, and only uses the network software that comes in the Windows 95 package. This can be a cheap and effective way to network an office. (To set up a peer-to-peer network, see page 6.)

- ❑ A *server* network may have larger computers as file servers, and will be linked by Windows NT or Novell Netware. Windows 95 PCs can connect into these networks. Setting up a server network is outside the scope of this book.

LAN – Local Area Network

A local area network may link together anything from 2 to 2,000 or more computers. The network will owned by one organisation, managed as a single unit and located on one site – though the site may be anything from a single office to a set of buildings scattered over a large campus.

Typically a LAN's users will have fairly free access to all its peripherals, and to the programs stored on the system. Access to its data may well be controlled by passwords, so that sensitive files can only be read and/or edited by authorised users.

On a LAN, most machines are workstations – desktop PCs on which users run their applications. Some act as servers, providing resources to others on the network.

- ● A **file server** holds data or program files that can be accessed by other machines.

- ● A **print server** has a printer attached to it. When files are sent to it for printing, they are first 'spooled' (stored) on its hard disk.

- ● A **comms server** has a modem attached. If it is a fax-modem, incoming faxes are stored on its hard disk.

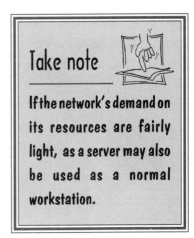

Take note

If the network's demand on its resources are fairly light, as a server may also be used as a normal workstation.

LAN standards

LANs are normally based on either the Ethernet or the Token Ring hardware and standards. These define the cards, cables and other network hardware, and the way that networked computers talk to each other at the electronic level.

Ethernet – widely used in small and large offices. The only essential hardware for an Ethernet LAN is a card to slot into each PC and cables to run between them.

Token Ring – a more robust means of networking, used where there is more chance of damage to cables. As well as cards and cables, these use control units, each of which handles the connections for up to 8 computers.

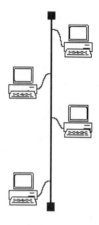

Two possible layouts for Ethernet networks – a central cable with spurs (above) or a 'daisy chain' with separate cables between each pair of computers (below). Both can be expanded by adding more cable at the ends.

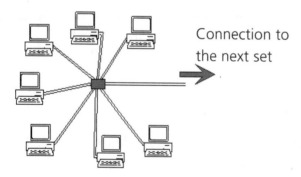

Connection to the next set

The layout of a Token Ring network. Data flows to each computer in turn, via the control unit. If a connection is broken, the unit bypasses it to keep the rest of the network intact.

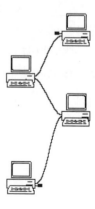

Take note

A Windows 95 network can be based on either Ethernet, Token Ring (or other) hardware.

WAN — Wide Area Network

A WAN may extend across the whole country, or even round the world.

Some WANs are private – owned and run by one company for its own needs. Supermarket chains use national WANs to track stock levels and arrange distribution to their many stores. Multi-national businesses, such as IBM, run their own world-wide WANs so that distant parts of the organisation can keep in close touch with each other.

Other WANs are public, opening their long-distance links to individuals or businesses. CompuServe, for example, has a network reaching into almost every country in the world, and into all major cities in North America and some European countries. One day, if Microsoft succeeds in its aims, MSN (the MicroSoft Network) will offer the same or greater coverage. Only those few computers that form the cores of these WANs are permanent parts of the networks – subscribers dial-up and link in when they need to.

Internetworks

An 'internetwork' links together LANs and WANs belonging to different organisations. The greatest of these networks is the Internet. We seem to be approaching the point where all the world's networks are linked into this, either as providers or users of its facilities.

Internetworks serve two main functions:

- fast, efficient communications between their users
- shared access to files – at least, to those held in public directories.

Peer-to-peer networking

Setting up a peer-to-peer network by daisy-chaining your computers requires a little extra hardware, but no special network software and no special skills. Once in place, it requires no special management and can be used competently by anyone who has read the first half of this –or a similar – book.

Adapter cards

For each computer you need an Ethernet adapter card. Cards suitable for PC networks can be obtained from your local computer dealer or any reputable mail order firm, and currently cost from £30 upwards. The more you pay, the better the performance, but if you only want to link a few PCs so that they can share a printer and transfer the occasional file, then the cheapest cards will do the job. If the network traffic is likely to be heavy, with users regularly accessing centrally-stored data, or sending many files for printing, then buy high performance cards.

To install a card, switch off the PC at the mains, undo the casing screws and open it up. The card should be pressed securely into a free expansion slot. Note the two sockets on the back of the card for the cable connections.

It should not matter which expansion slot you use, nor should you need to change any of the settings on your PC. If,after you have set up the network at Windows 95 level you cannot make it work, then – after you have double-checked everything else and it still won't work – try the card in a different slot.

Take note

If a PC's expansion slots are all occupied, or you want to link in a laptop, you can get adaptors to plug into the parallel port.

Cables

You need cables to link each computer to the next. To work out the lengths, take a ball of string and run it out along the track the cable must take – around the walls and over doorways, if necessary. Measure the string and allow an extra metre, just in case – you can loop overlong cables, but you cannot stretch short ones. The cables need connectors at either end. Fitting them is a specialist job, but your local dealer should be able to make up cables to your requirements. Depending upon the length, they should cost around £10 to £20 each.

To install the cables, simply fit one end into the network card of a PC, lay it out along a safe track – fastening into place with cable clips – and plug it into the next machine.

Lastly you need two terminators, one at each end of the daisy chain. They fit into the empty sockets in the network cards and complete the circuit.

Network software

The card will normally be accompanied a disk, containing software to manage the low-level network communications and a program to install it for you. Run the installation and follow any on-screen instructions.

You are now ready to set up the Windows 95 side of the network.

Take note

You must not lay cable where it can be trodden on or tripped over. If it has to cross a pathway, then you will need thick rubber cable covers to protect it.

Adding a network adapter

Ethernet adapter cards will handle one aspect of the communications between your computers, but another adapter – the *Client for Microsoft Networks* – is needed to run a Windows 95 network. This software is available on the Windows 95 distribution disks or CD-ROM, and is installed through the Network icon on the Control Panel.

You must work through these steps on every computer on your network.

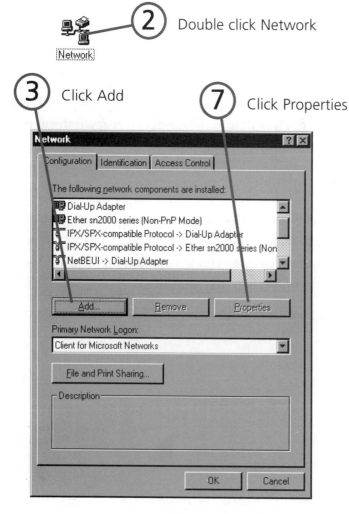

Double click Network

Click Add

Click Properties

Basic steps

1 Open the **Start** menu and select **Settings** then **Control Panel**

2 Double click the **Network** icon

3 Click [Add...]

4 At the **Component Type** panel, select **Client** and click [Add...]

5 At the **Network Client** panel, select **Microsoft**, then **Client for Microsoft Networks**.

6 If the software was not loaded when Windows 95 was installed, you will be prompted for the distribution disk.

7 Back at the **Network** panel, select the new Client item and click [Properties]

8 Clear the **Logon to Windows NT domain** checkbox.

9 Select **Logon and restore network connections**.

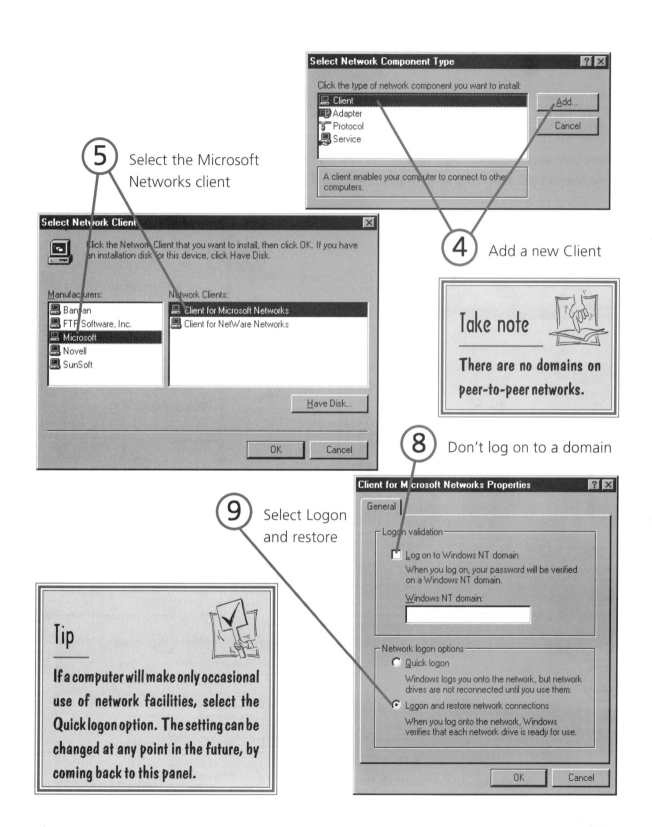

Select Network Component Type

Click the type of network component you want to install:

- Client
- Adapter
- Protocol
- Service

Add...

Cancel

A client enables your computer to connect to other computers.

(5) Select the Microsoft Networks client

(4) Add a new Client

Select Network Client

Click the Network Client that you want to install, then click OK. If you have an installation disk for this device, click Have Disk.

Manufacturers:
- Banyan
- FTP Software, Inc.
- Microsoft
- Novell
- SunSoft

Network Clients:
- Client for Microsoft Networks
- Client for NetWare Networks

Have Disk...

OK   Cancel

Take note

There are no domains on peer-to-peer networks.

(8) Don't log on to a domain

(9) Select Logon and restore

Client for Microsoft Networks Properties

General

Logon validation

☐ Log on to Windows NT domain

When you log on, your password will be verified on a Windows NT domain.

Windows NT domain:

Network logon options

○ Quick logon

Windows logs you onto the network, but network drives are not reconnected until you use them.

◉ Logon and restore network connections

When you log onto the network, Windows verifies that each network drive is ready for use.

OK   Cancel

Tip

If a computer will make only occasional use of network facilities, select the Quick logon option. The setting can be changed at any point in the future, by coming back to this panel.

Identifying the computer

Each computer in the network must be given a name and a description. The more computers there are, the more important it is to ensure that they are clearly identified – when the users are accessing the network's resources, they should be able to tell at a glance which computer they need to link to.

1 On the **Network** panel, switch to the **Identification** tab.

2 Enter names for the **Computer** and the **Workgroup**, and type in a short **Description**.

3 Switch back to the **Configuration** tab for the next stage of the installation.

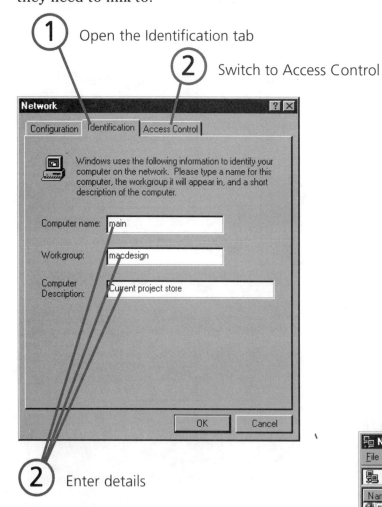

① Open the Identification tab

② Switch to Access Control

② Enter details

Names and descriptions are shown in the Network Neighboorhood displays (see page 20 for more in this.)

Take note

A Workgroup name is essential, even on a small network where all the computers/users form one group. The name can be anything – but must be the same on all linked machines.

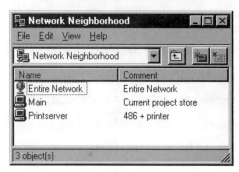

Basic steps

1 Click [File and Print Sharing...]

2 Check the **files** and **printer** options as appropriate and click [OK]

3 On the **Access Control** tab select **Share-level access control** – the only viable option on a peer-to-peer network.

4 Click [OK] to close the panel

Sharing resources

If the computer has any resources – files, printers or whatever – that are to be used over the network, you must turn on the sharing options on the Properties panel. Exactly which resources are to be shared, and how, will be estfablished at the next stage.

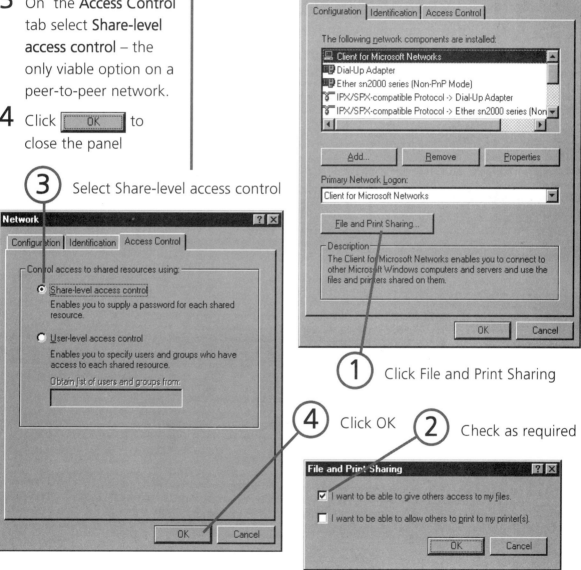

③ Select Share-level access control

Network [?][X]

Configuration | Identification | Access Control

Control access to shared resources using:

◉ Share-level access control
Enables you to supply a password for each shared resource.

○ User-level access control
Enables you to specify users and groups who have access to each shared resource.

Obtain list of users and groups from:

[OK] [Cancel]

Network [?][X]

Configuration | Identification | Access Control

The following network components are installed:

- 🖳 Client for Microsoft Networks
- 📇 Dial-Up Adapter
- 📇 Ether sn2000 series (Non-PnP Mode)
- IPX/SPX-compatible Protocol -> Dial-Up Adapter
- IPX/SPX-compatible Protocol -> Ether sn2000 series (Non

[Add...] [Remove] [Properties]

Primary Network Logon:

Client for Microsoft Networks

[File and Print Sharing...]

Description
The Client for Microsoft Networks enables you to connect to other Microsoft Windows computers and servers and use the files and printers shared on them.

[OK] [Cancel]

① Click File and Print Sharing

④ Click OK   ② Check as required

File and Print Sharing [?][X]

☑ I want to be able to give others access to my files.

☐ I want to be able to allow others to print to my printer(s).

[OK] [Cancel]

Access control

You will want to make some files accessible to all the network's users, but you may want to limit access to other files. Some will be confidential; some will be crucially important and must be protected from accidental damage.

Windows 95 lets you set which drives or folders are to be shared, and the nature of the sharing. *Read-only* sharing will allow other users to run a program or view the data in a file, but not change or delete it. With *Full* sharing, other users have as much control over the file as if it was on their own machine. Shared drives and folders can be password protected, to restrict access.

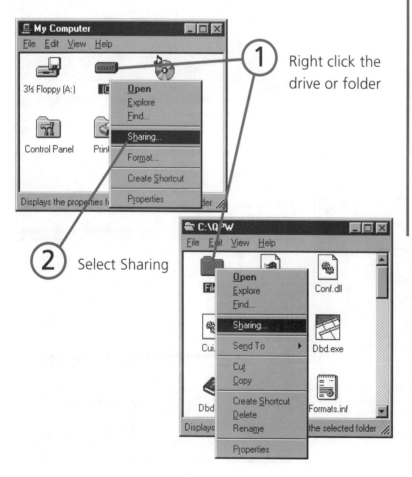

Right click the drive or folder

Select Sharing

1 In **My Computer** or **Explorer**, right click the drive or folder to be shared.

2 Select **Sharing** from its short menu.

3 On the **Sharing** tab, select **Shared As**.

4 Give the drive or folder a meaningful **Share name** – adding a **Comment** if useful

5 Select the **Access type**

6 Enter a **Password**, or leave it blank if no protection is needed.

7 Confirm the password by typing it again.

Take note

If you select access to Depend on Password, you will have to give different passwords for Read-only and Full Access

A shared resource
can be closed off
again at any point

③ Set Shared As

A drive may be left as a letter if
the computer is clearly identified

④ Identify it clearly

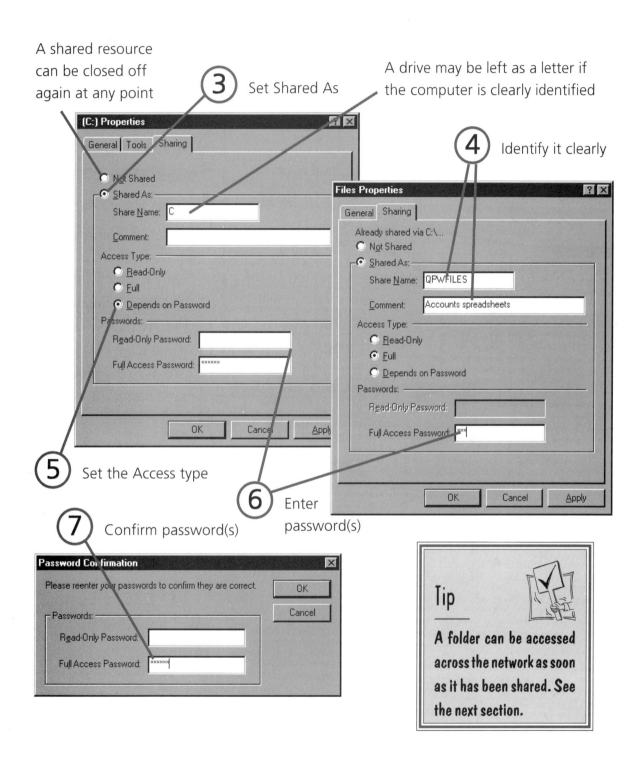

⑤ Set the Access type

⑥ Enter
password(s)

⑦ Confirm password(s)

A folder can be accessed
across the network as soon
as it has been shared. See
the next section.

Tip

Sharing a printer

To share a printer over the network you follow much the same steps as for sharing a folder. The setup must be done on the computer attached to the printer.

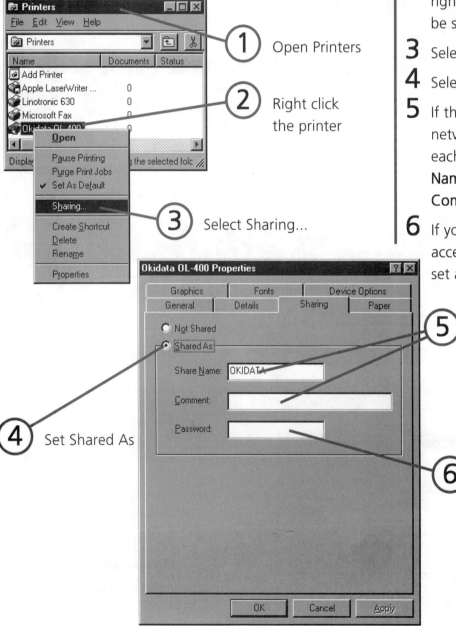

Open Printers

Right click the printer

Select Sharing...

Set Shared As

Give a Name (and Comment)

Set a Password if needed

1 Click **Start** and select **Settings** then **Printers**.

2 At the **Printers** folder right click the printer to be shared.

3 Select **Sharing**.

4 Select **Shared As**.

5 If there are several networked printer, give each an identifying **Name** – adding a **Comment** if useful.

6 If you want to restrict access to the printer, set a **Password**.

14

Basic steps

1 Open the printer's **Properties** panel.

2 Switch to the **General** tab.

3 Drop down the **Separator page** list and select **Full** or **Simple**.

or

4 Click [Browse...] and select a WMF file.

5 Click [OK]

Separator pages

When two or more people are sending files to the same printer, the printer will not get confused about which belongs to whom, but the users might. To save confusion, you can set the printer to produce a separator page before each file.

● The **Simple** separator shows the name of the file, the user and the time of printing – all in plain text.

● The **Full** separator also shows the user details, but in large type and decorated with a Windows 95 logo.

● You can use a WMF (Windows MetaFile drawing) file instead – it may make a striking divider, but will not carry any user details.

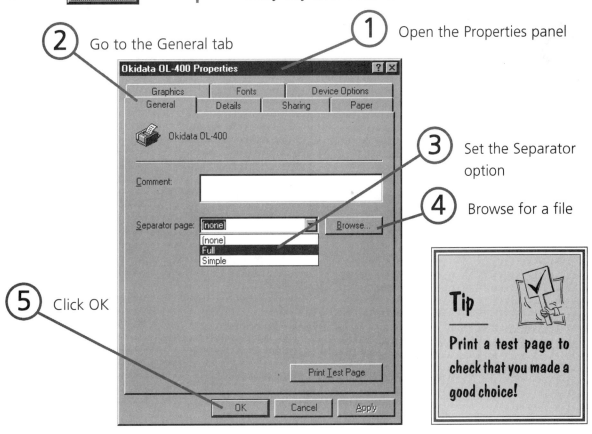

② Go to the General tab

① Open the Properties panel

③ Set the Separator option

④ Browse for a file

⑤ Click OK

Tip

Print a test page to check that you made a good choice!

15

Adding a network printer

The Add printer Wizard is used to link to a networked printer. The routine is almost identical to installing a new local printer.

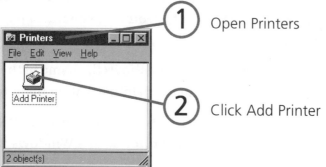

① Open Printers

② Click Add Printer

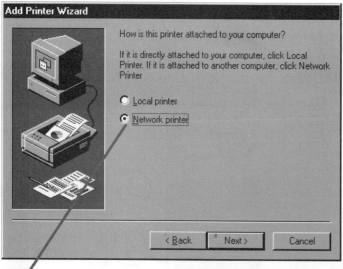

④ Select Network printer

Take note

You must use **Add printer** on each computer for each printer to be accessed over the network.

1 Click **Start** and select **Settings** then **Printers**.

2 At the **Printers** folder, click **Add Printer**.

3 Work through the Wizard, clicking `Next >` after each panel and `Finish` at the end.

4 At the first decision panel, select **Network printer**.

5 At the next panel, click `Browse...`.

6 In the **Browse** display, open the computer's folder, select the printer and click `OK`

7 If you want to **print from DOS programs**, select the option.

8 Edit the printer **Name** to identify it and **set as the default** if required.

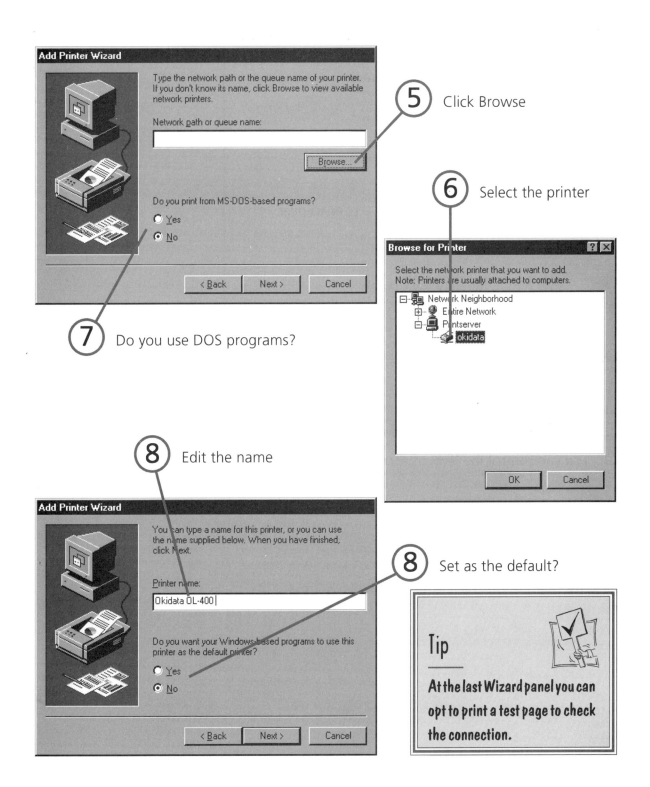

Add Printer Wizard

Type the network path or the queue name of your printer. If you don't know its name, click Browse to view available network printers.

Network path or queue name:

[   ]

Browse...

Do you print from MS-DOS-based programs?

○ Yes
● No

< Back   Next >   Cancel

⑤ Click Browse

⑥ Select the printer

Browse for Printer

Select the network printer that you want to add.
Note: Printers are usually attached to computers.

- Network Neighborhood
  - Entire Network
  - Printserver
    - okidata

OK   Cancel

⑦ Do you use DOS programs?

⑧ Edit the name

⑧ Set as the default?

Add Printer Wizard

You can type a name for this printer, or you can use the name supplied below. When you have finished, click Next.

Printer name:

[Okidata OL-400]

Do you want your Windows-based programs to use this printer as the default printer?

○ Yes
● No

< Back   Next >   Cancel

Tip

At the last Wizard panel you can opt to print a test page to check the connection.

17

Summary

- ❑ A **network** is a set of computers, connected together so that they can share their resources.

- ❑ A **Local Area Network** is one run on one site by one organisation.

- ❑ **Wide Area Networks** allow remote communications and resource-sharing.

- ❑ With Windows 95 you can set up a **peer-to-peer network**. Unlike a server network, this has no single controlling computer.

- ❑ The only **additional hardware** needed for a peer-to-peer network are adapter cards for each machine, plus cables to link them.

- ❑ Each computer must have a **name** which clearly identifies it.

- ❑ **Files and printers** attached to computers can be opened for **sharing** with others on the network.

- ❑ You can **control the level of access** to files, and set passwords if required.

- ❑ Shared printers can be set to output **separator pages** to identify each printout.

- ❑ On each computer that is to access a shared printer, you must run the **Add printer** routine for that printer.

2 LAN files and folders

Network Neighborhood

Windows 95 views the network as another folder. It is usually simplest to access it through the Network Neighborhood icon on the Desktop. This produces a 'My Computer' style window. I find it useful to turn on the Toolbar and set the View mode to Details, so that the Descriptions are visible.

Basic steps

1 Click

2 Open the **View** menu and turn on **Toolbar**

3 Select the **Details** view

② Turn on the Toolbar

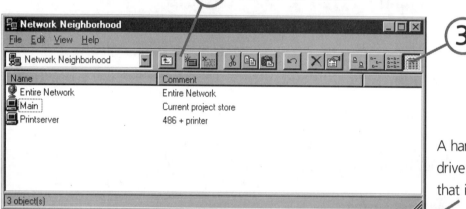

③ Use Details view

A hand beneath a drive or folder shows that it is shared

The network can also be viewed through Explorer. This shows the structure clearly – in the All Folders pane – and gives easier access to sub-folders. With Network Neighborhood you may have to open four or five windows to get to the level you want.

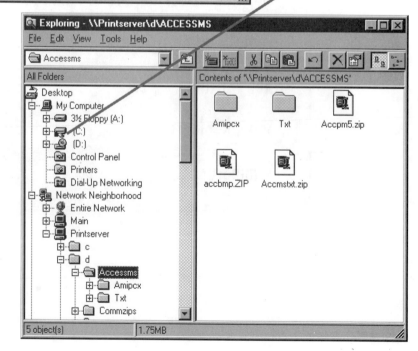

Basic steps

Accessing a folder

1 Open **Network Neighborhood**

2 Double click a computer's icon to open its window

3 Double click a folder to open it

4 Enter the password, if required.

Those networked drives and folders that have been shared – and to which you have the passwords – can be treated as extensions of your own system. You can copy files from (and possibly to) these folders, and run programs that are stored on remote computers. The techniques are almost identical to those for working on your own machine.

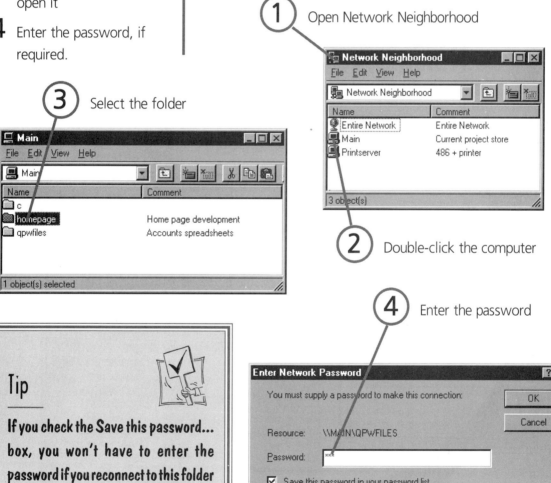

① Open Network Neighborhood

③ Select the folder

② Double-click the computer

④ Enter the password

Tip

If you check the Save this password... box, you won't have to enter the password if you reconnect to this folder later in the same working session.

Copying over the network

When you first set up the network, there are likely to be a number of programs and data files that need copying or moving from one machine to another.

Take note

As long as you have at least Read access to a networked folder, you can copy its files — or the whole folder. If you have Full access, you can also copy files into it.

1 Work through **Network Neighborhood** to bring the folder or files into view

2 Use **My Computer** or **Explorer** to display the target folder or drive.

❏ Copying

3 Drag the file or folder across to the target

❏ Moving

4 Hold down the right button as you drag then select **Move Here**

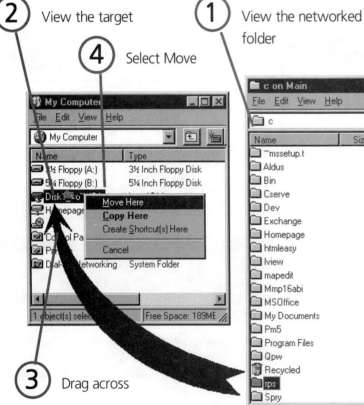

② View the target

④ Select Move

① View the networked folder

③ Drag across

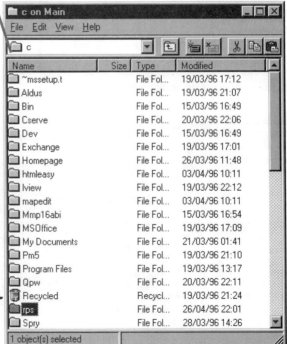

Basic steps

1 Use the application's **File – Open** command

2 Go back up to the Desktop if necessary

3 Work down through the structure

4 Open the file as usual.

In applications written for Windows 95, you can access the network from the Open dialog box. Work through the levels to the right folder, and you can open the file as if it were in a folder on your computer.

This only works with true Windows 95 applications.

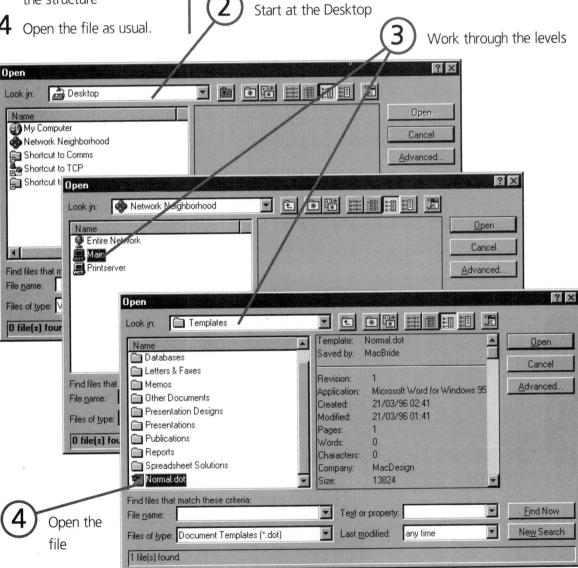

② Start at the Desktop

③ Work through the levels

④ Open the file

Mapping drives

On a Windows 95 network, you can connect to a remote (shared) drive or folder so that it appears as a drive on the local computer. Mapped drives can be viewed through My Computer or Explorer, but more importantly they can be accessed by those older Windows applications that do not support the Network Neighborhood.

Basic steps

❑ **Mapping a drive**

1 In **Network Neighborhood** find the drive or folder to be mapped.

2 Right click to open the menu and select **Map Network Drive**.

3 Drop down the **Drive** list and select an unused drive letter

4 Check **Reconnect at logon** if you want to have the same connection in later work sessions

5 Click [OK]

6 Give the **password** if prompted.

❑ **Using a mapped drive**

7 Use the application's **File – Open** command to get the Open dialog box

8 Drop down the **Drives** list and select the mapped drive.

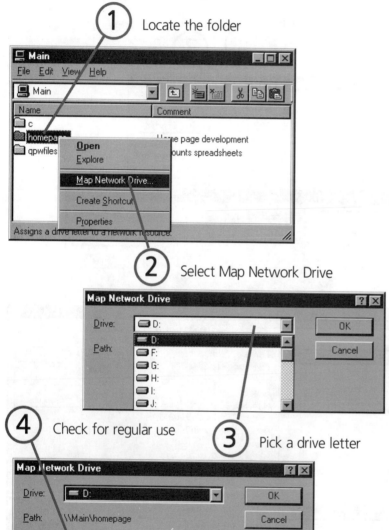

Locate the folder

Select Map Network Drive

Pick a drive letter

Check for regular use

24

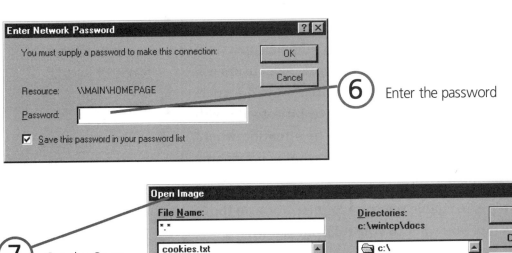

⑥ Enter the password

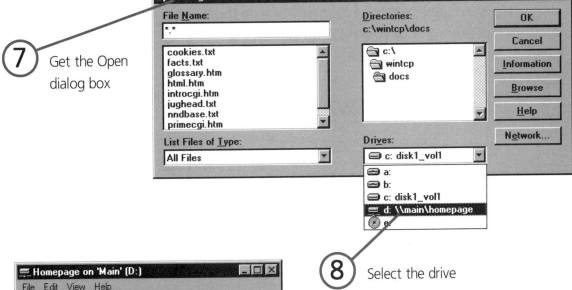

⑦ Get the Open dialog box

⑧ Select the drive

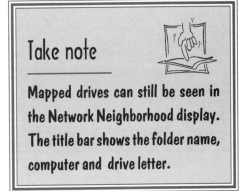

Take note

Mapped drives can still be seen in the Network Neighborhood display. The title bar shows the folder name, computer and drive letter.

Remote administration

This is probably more important on a server network, where there is a system administrator who has oversight of the network. On a peer-to-peer network, most users will take responsibility for their own computers and – apart from sharing files and printers – have little to do with other machines. However, there will be situation where you may need to know and to control what is happening elsewhere on the network.

The first step is to enable remote administration on those computers that you want to control from elsewhere.

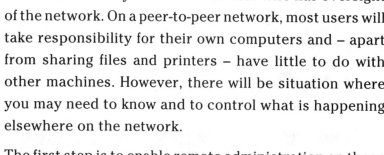

② Open Password Properties

③ Switch to Remote Administration

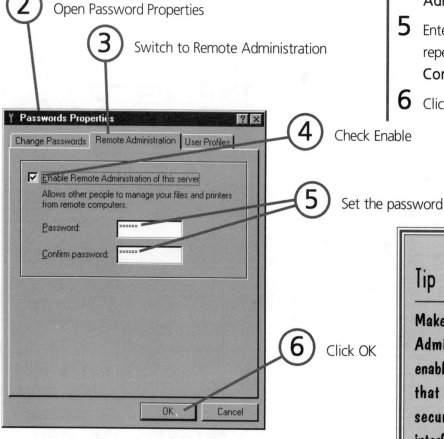

④ Check Enable

⑤ Set the password

⑥ Click OK

1 From the **Start** button, select **Settings** then **Control Panel**

2 Click

3 At the **Password Properties** panel switch to the **Remote Administration** tab

4 Check **Enable Remote Adminstration**

5 Enter a **Password**, repeating it in the **Confirm** slot.

6 Click [OK   ]

Tip

Make sure that Remote Administration is not enabled on any computer that you want to keep secure from outside interference.

Basic steps

Installing Net watcher

❏ Have your WIndows 95 CD-ROM or installation disks ready.

1 Open the **Control Panel**

2 Click ![Add/Remove Programs icon] Add/Remove Programs

3 Switch to the **Windows Setup** tab

4 Select **Accessories**

5 Click [Details...]

6 Tick **Net Watcher**

7 Click [OK]

Net watcher enables you to view and control events on those other computers that have had Remote Administration enabled. It should be present on your Accessories – System Tools menu. If not, install it now.

③ Go to Windows Setup

④ Select Accessories

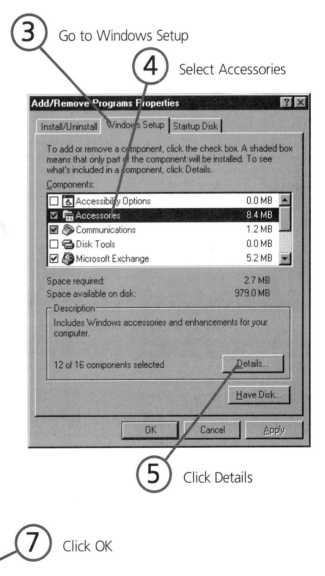

⑤ Click Details

⑥ Check Net Watcher

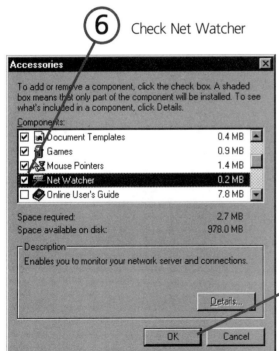

⑦ Click OK

Net watching

Net Watcher allows you to monitor the usage of any computer that provides services – shared folders or printer – to the network.

You can view the server's activity in terms of its Connections (users), Shared Folders or Open Files. Each view offers a set of appropriate commands.

Basic steps

1 Open **Network Neighborhood**.

2 Right click on a machine's icon to open its short menu.

3 Select **Properties**.

4 Open the **Tools** tab.

5 Click [Net Watcher]

6 Open the **View** menu and select a **by...** style

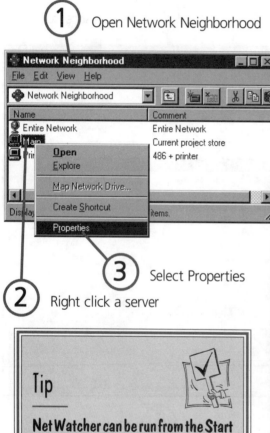

Open Network Neighborhood

① Open Network Neighborhood

③ Select Properties

② Right click a server

④ Switch to the Tools tab

⑤ Click Net Watcher

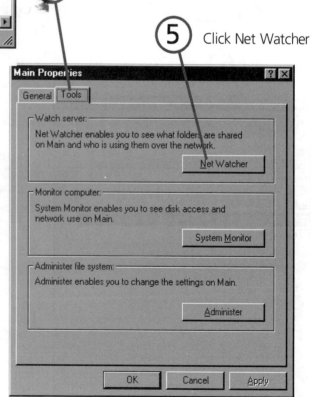

Tip

Net Watcher can be run from the Start menu (in the Accessories – System Tools folder). You then use the Administer – Select Server command to pick a computer. It is usually simpler to start from Network neighborhood.

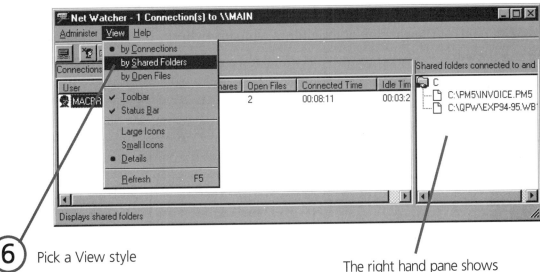

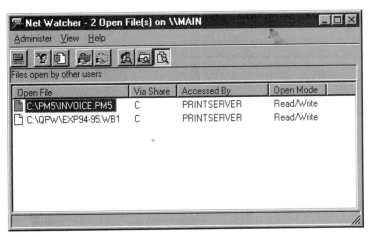

(6) Pick a View style

The right hand pane shows details of shared folders and open files. This can be tucked away if not needed.

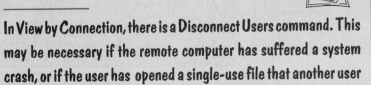

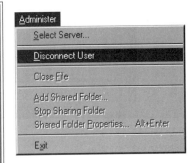

Take note

In View by Connection, there is a Disconnect Users command. This may be necessary if the remote computer has suffered a system crash, or if the user has opened a single-use file that another user needs to access, and the first cannot be contacted to close it properly.

29

Shared folders

If Remote Administration has been enabled on a computer, you can control the sharing of its folders from elsewhere on the network.

1 Run **Net Watcher** and switch to **View – by Shared Folders**.

❑ Sharing a folder

2 Open the **Administer** menu and select **Add Shared Folder**.

3 Enter the **Path** to the folder

or

4 Click [Browse...] and select the folder from the display.

5 Click [OK]

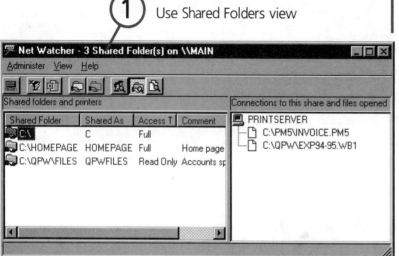

Use Shared Folders view

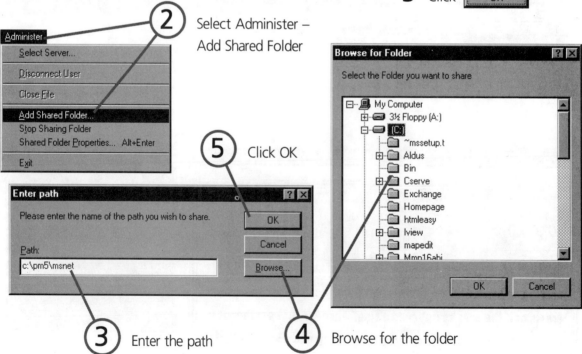

③ Enter the path

④ Browse for the folder

⑤ Click OK

Closing a folder

1 Check that the folder is not in use!

2 Open the **Administer** menu and select **Stop Sharing Folder**.

2 Click [Yes] to confirm.

If you want to stop sharing a folder, the process is just as quick and easy as starting, except that you must watch out for active users. If someone is working on a file in a shared folder when you close it down, they will not e able to save their work.

(1) Check the connections

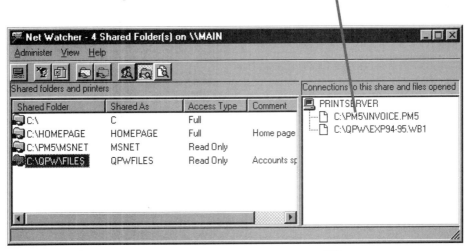

Take note

You can stop sharing a folder, even if it is in use, though the user may not appreciate it.

(2) Select Administer – Stop Sharing Folder

(3) Click Yes

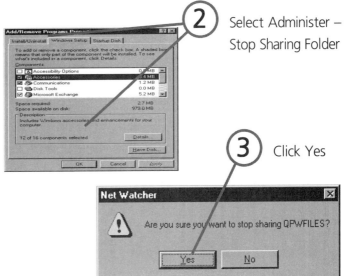

Summary

❑ **Network Neighborhood** gives you the same view of the network that My Computer does of your own machine.

❑ You can also view the network through **Explorer**.

❑ **Copying files** over the network is the same as copying them between drives or folders of a single computer – though you must have the necessary access to read or store files.

❑ In **Windows 95 applications**, you can open networked folders through the normal Open dialog box.

❑ You must **map networked drives** onto drive letters to be able to access them from within older applications.

❑ If **remote administration** is enabled, a computer – and access to its files – can be controlled from another elsewhere on the nework.

❑ With **Net watcher** you can monitor the levels of use of networked resources.

3 Working on the LAN

Potential problems

Once the network – and all the applications used on the network – are set up properly, you shouldn't have any problems at all. However, you will no doubt meet some in moving towards that happy state.

Data files

If several users are to read and edit the same files, this can only be done safely with network versions of applications.

Look what can happen with single-user applications, if two people try to edit the same file.

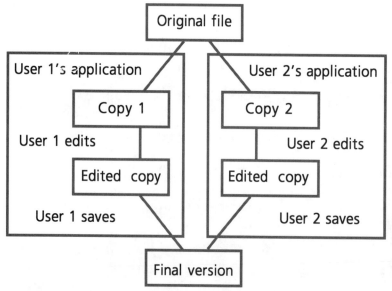

They both open the original file and have a copy in memory, in their applications. They edit their copies, but when they save, user 2's copy will overwrite the version that User 1 has just saved – wiping out those edits.

Network versions of applications either update the central copy of the file as it is edited, or restrict access so that only one person can edit at a time – though others may be able to openthe file for reading.

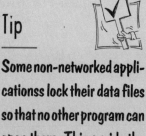

Tip

Some non-networked applicationss lock their data files so that no other program can open them. This avoids the problems that can be caused by simultaneous editing – by not allowing it!

When you network your computers, network your key applications to match.

Running programs

Take note

With commercial software, you may well need an extension to its license to run the software legally over your network. Some licenses restrict use to one machine only.

You can run programs that are stored on remote computer, on your local machine. They may be a little slower when you first start, when you call up the help pages and when you access certain routines for the first time, as files have to be copied over the network into your computer's memory. Otherwise, the performance should be as good as it would be if the software was on the local hard disk.

There are two problems that you are likely to meet:

● When the software was installed, essential DLL files may have been stored in the WINDOWS or WINDOWS\SYSTEM folder. When you try to run the program, it will look in your folders for those files – and fail to find them. You will see an error message if this happens. The solution is to copy the named files into the equivalent folder on your own hard disk.

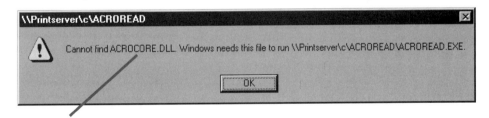

\\Printserver\c\ACROREAD

⚠ Cannot find ACROCORE.DLL. Windows needs this file to run \\Printserver\c\ACROREAD\ACROREAD.EXE.

OK

Use Find to locate the missing file on the remote computer, then copy it to a folder with the same name on your computer.

● When you first save a file, the default folder may well be on the remote computer. This is not a major problem, as you can work your way back to your own machine and save there. However, if you are going to use this software regularly, make life simple for yourself. Set up a shortcut to the program and specify your own default folder. (See next page.)

Networked shortcuts

Tracking down files over the network can be hard work, but it only takes a moment to create a shortcut. Do it once, and you can run a remote program from your Desktop with a click of a button.

1 Work through **Network Neighborhood** to open the program's folder.

2 Hold the right button and drag the program icon onto your Desktop.

3 Select **Create Shortcut Here** from the menu.

4 Right click on the shortcut icon to open its **Properties** panel.

5 On the **Shortcut** tab, set the default folder for data files in the **Starts in** slot.

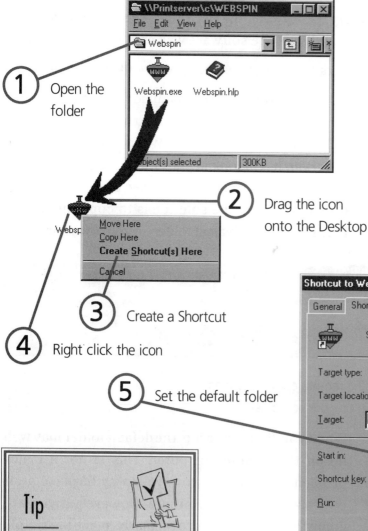

① Open the folder

② Drag the icon onto the Desktop

③ Create a Shortcut

④ Right click the icon

⑤ Set the default folder

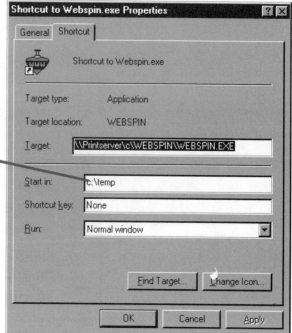

Tip

You can also create shortcuts to folders on the network.

36

Basic steps

1 From the **Start** button, select **Settings** then **Printers**.

2 Right click on the printer's icon and select **Properties**.

3 Work through the tabs and change the settings as required.

When you send a file to be printed, it is first stored (spooled) on the attached computer. Spooled files are normally printed in the order that they were received – though the computer's user can adjust the order. Spooling prevents clashes if two people try to print at once.

You can access a network printer's Properties page to check or adjust its setup as required. Any changes made to the settings only affect the printouts from that computer – the same printer can print to A4 paper from one machine and Envelopes from another.

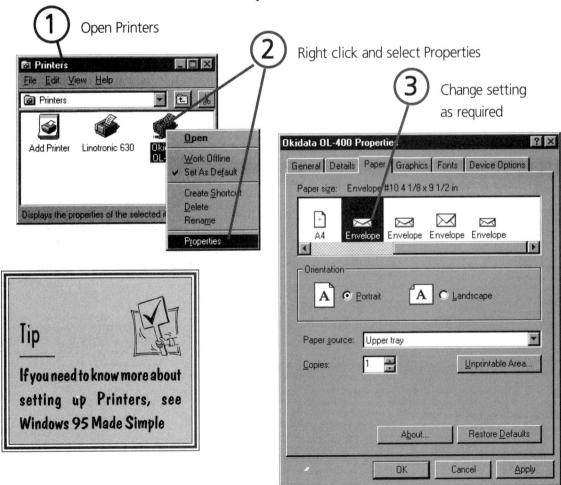

① Open Printers

② Right click and select Properties

③ Change setting as required

Tip

If you need to know more about setting up Printers, see Windows 95 Made Simple

37

WinChat

WinChat lets you have interactive "conversations" with other people on your local network. The software is part of the standard Windows 95 package, though easily overlooked as it does not appear in the Setup options.

Basic steps

❏ **Installation**

1 Run **Add/Remove Programs**, opening the **Windows Setup** tab.

2 Click [Have Disk...]

3 At the **Install from Disk** dialog, [Browse...] for the folder – on the CD-ROM it is in the Other/ Chat folder.

4 At the **Have Disk** dialog tick the checkbox and click [Install]

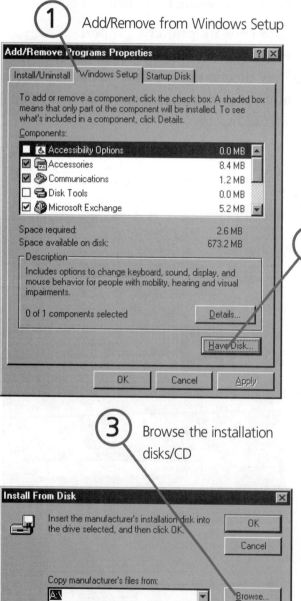

① Add/Remove from Windows Setup

② Click Have Disk

③ Browse the installation disks/CD

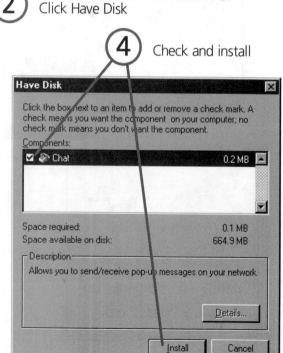

④ Check and install

Basic steps

Using Chat

❑ Calling for a Chat

1 Click [icon] and type the name of the machine – not the person – you want to talk to.

❑ Responding

2 When the "phone" rings, click [icon]

3 Type into the top – or the left – pane. The other person's typing appears in the lower/ right pane.

❑ Ending the call

4 Click [icon] to end the call and [X] to clear your pane, then minimise Chat.

If you want to chat or be chatted to, you must have Chat running – it can be minimized when not in active use. Add Winchat to your Startup group if you use it a lot.

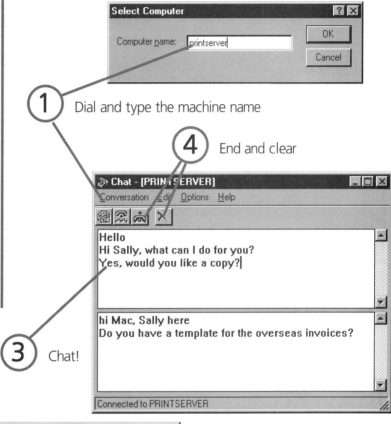

(1) Dial and type the machine name

(4) End and clear

(3) Chat!

(2) Take the call

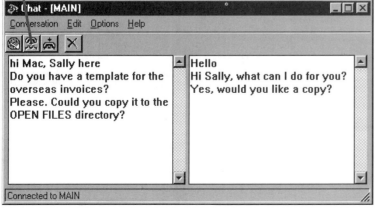

You can set Options to split the screen down or across. You can also select fonts and the background colour if you like!

Sharing Clipbooks

Clipbook, like WinChat, is another Windows 95 utility that is often ignored. It is basically an extension of the Clipboard, that allows you to store any number of items captured with Edit–Cut or Copy. More relevant for us, it also allows you to cut and paste items over a network.

❏ **Installation**

Follow the steps on page 38, opening the **Other/Clipbook** folder.

❏ **Storing in the Clipbook**

1 Cut or copy from an application as normal

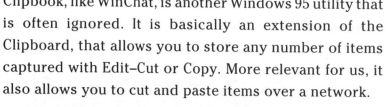

② Paste into the Clipbook

2 With the **Local Clipbook** active, open the **Edit** menu and select **Paste**.

3 Type in a name for the 'page' that will hold the item.

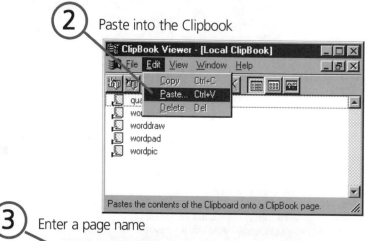

③ Enter a page name

④ Tick Share now

4 Tick **Share item now**, and set access and passwords as required in the following dialog.

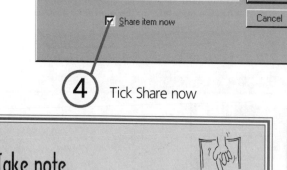

Take note

The Clipbook cannot handle all types of data. For example, Word formatted text and drawings copy well, but WordPad text loses its formatting. Do not try to copy bitmaps – they crash the system!

Stop sharing

Share   Delete item   View modes

Basic steps

❏ **Copying over the LAN**

1 Open the **File** menu and select **Connect...**

2 Type in the name of the computer

3 Open the **Window** menu and select the remote **Clipbook**

4 Click on the item you want, then use **Edit– Copy** to copy it to the ordinary Clipboard.

5 Go into the application and use **Edit–Paste** as normal.

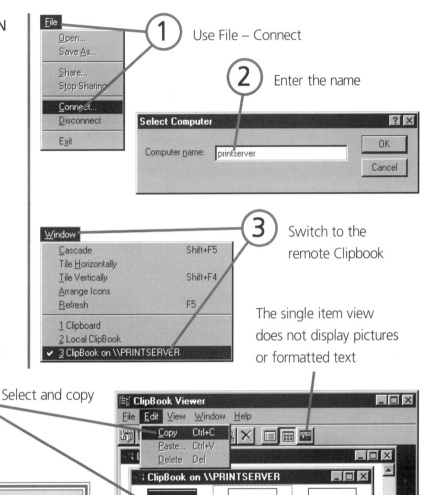

① Use File – Connect

② Enter the name

③ Switch to the remote Clipbook

The single item view does not display pictures or formatted text

④ Select and copy

Tip

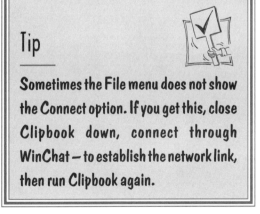

Sometimes the File menu does not show the Connect option. If you get this, close Clipbook down, connect through WinChat – to establish the network link, then run Clipbook again.

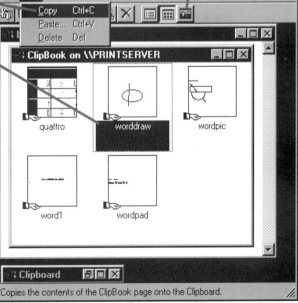

Summary

❑ You may hit problems when you try to share data files from single-user versions of applications. You should only use network versions to handle shared data.

❑ You can run programs that are stored on remote computers, though it may sometimes be necessary to copy some DLL files onto your own system.

❑ By setting up n etworked shortcuts you can get easy access to programs and folders on remote machines.

❑ Files are spooled on the computers of networked printers, before being printed. These computers must have space on their hard disk for this temporary storage.

❑ You can set up your own options for networked printers. This will not affect other people's output.

❑ WinChat allows network users to have real-time 'conversations'.

❑ By using Clipbooks, people can copy and paste data across the network – though not all forms of data can be copied in this way.

4 Preparing for e-mail

Communicate!

You can use Microsoft Exchange to handle all of your electronic communications both within the local office network, and out to the world beyond.

- The text that you send can be formatted, using colour or different fonts and styles to add impact to your messages.

- Spreadsheets, databases, graphics and other documents can be embedded in the messages, and transmitted with them, or included as a link to a file in a shared folder.

Precisely what forms of communication are available to you depend upon the setup of your system.

- To communicate with other users on a LAN, one computer must have a Post office set up on it (see page 50), and each user must install Mail.

- For e-mail over the Internet, there must be a modem either attached to your machine or shared over the network. Dial Up Networking must be installed (see page 56) and you must also have an account with MSN (MicroSoft Network) or another service provider.

- To send faxes via Exchange, there must be a fax/modem either on your machine or on the LAN.

Take note

The examples in this book all use MSN as the external communications service, but Exchange works well with the connection to any Internet service provider. (See page 47.)

44

Basic steps

1 Have your Windows 95 installation disks ready.

2 Open the **Control Panel** and double click **Add/Remove Programs**.

3 Switch to the **Windows Setup** tab.

4 Select **Exchange**

5 click Details...

6 Tick the **Exchange** box.

7 If you are on a LAN, also tick the **Mail Services** box.

8 Click OK and follow the prompts.

If Exchange is not installed in you computer(s), now is tthe time to do it. Use Add/Remove Programs, as usual, to get the software in place, then run through the Wizard that will configure it to your system.

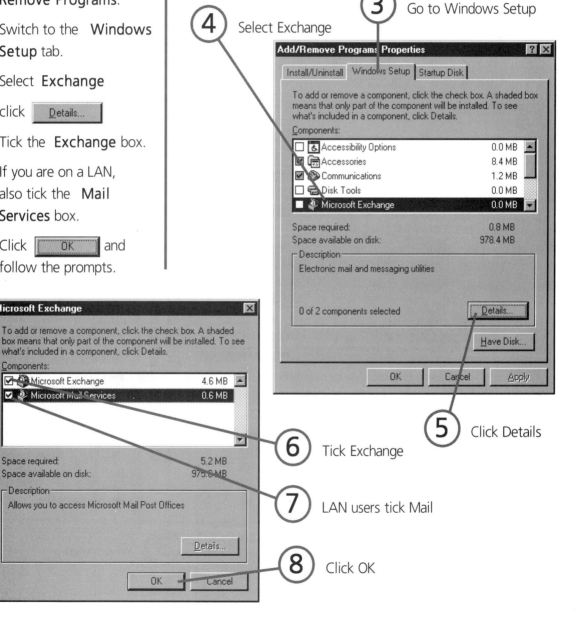

③ Go to Windows Setup

④ Select Exchange

⑤ Click Details

⑥ Tick Exchange

⑦ LAN users tick Mail

⑧ Click OK

Inbox Setup Wizard

The Inbox Setup Wizard configures the whole of your mail system, not just the part that handles incoming mail. Most panels are self-explanatory.

Basic steps

1 Turn on **Microsoft Mail** (local network) and **Internet Mail** as required.

2 Enter, or browse for, the **Path** to the LAN's Post Office.

3 Select your **Name** from the list.

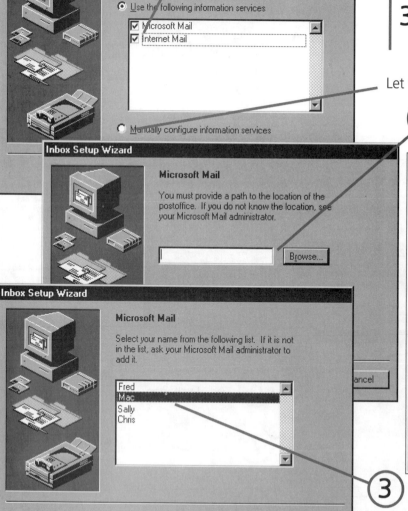

① Check as required

Let the Wizard do it

② Set the PO path

③ Who are you?

Tip

If the post office and your e-mail account have not yet been set up (see page 52), enter any folder and any name — you must enter something! — and correct them later through the Exchange Properties panel.

46

Basic steps

1 Select **Modem** for the connection method.

2 Click

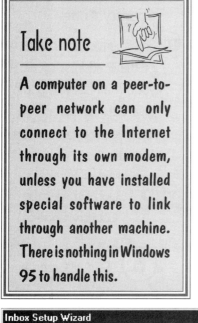

Internet Mail

The remaining panels of the Wizard configure your connection to the Internet.

You will need details of the account with the **service provider** to complete this. Dig out the paperwork, or run any existing e-mail software and read the details of its configuration panels – you can run another program without quitting the Wizard.

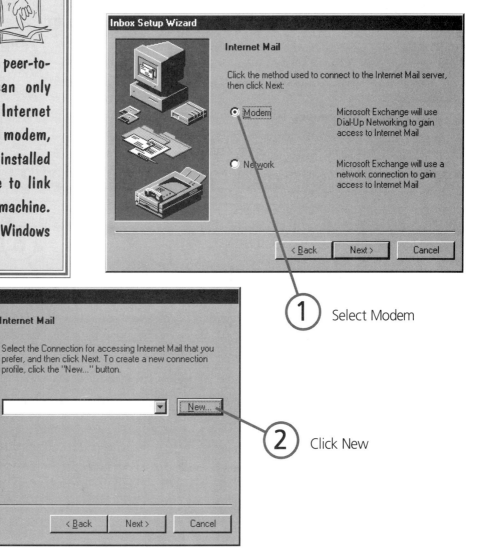

① Select Modem

② Click New

Basic steps

3 Type a **name** for the connection

4 Check that the **modem** is correctly selected.

5 Enter the **phone number**, including the **Country Code**!

6 Select either the name or the IP address of your **mail server**, and give their details as specified by your provider.

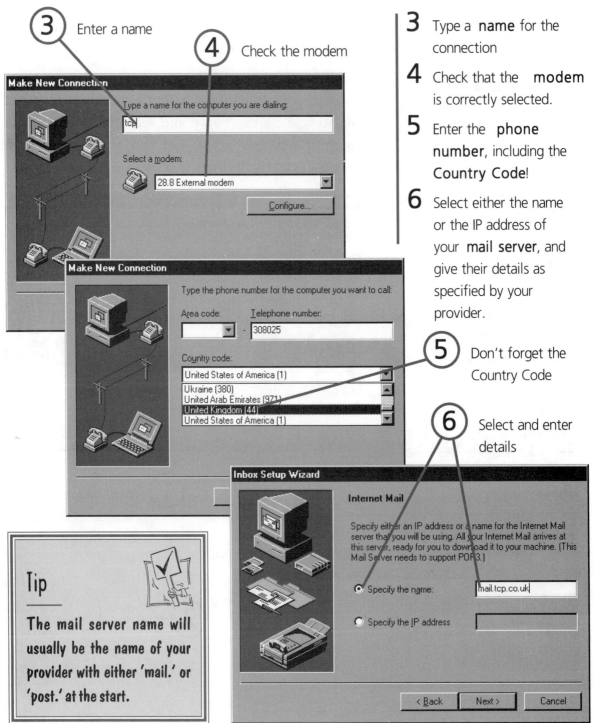

③ Enter a name

④ Check the modem

Make New Connection

Type a name for the computer you are dialing:

tcp

Select a modem:

28.8 External modem

Configure...

Make New Connection

Type the phone number for the computer you want to call:

Area code: Telephone number:

308025

Country code:

United States of America (1)

Ukraine (380)
United Arab Emirates (971)
United Kingdom (44)
United States of America (1)

⑤ Don't forget the Country Code

⑥ Select and enter details

Inbox Setup Wizard

Internet Mail

Specify either an IP address or a name for the Internet Mail server that you will be using. All your Internet Mail arrives at this server, ready for you to download it to your machine. (This Mail Server needs to support POP3.)

◉ Specify the name: mail.tcp.co.uk

○ Specify the IP address

< Back   Next >   Cancel

Tip

The mail server name will usually be the name of your provider with either 'mail.' or 'post.' at the start.

48

7 Select **Off-line** if you want to control when mail is sent, using the Remote Mail tool; otherwise leave it on **Automatic**.

8 Give your **e-mail address** and name – these identify the mail you send.

9 Give the name and password for the **mailbox account** – these will be used to log onto the server.

10 Click [Next >] for the final panel, then [Finish]

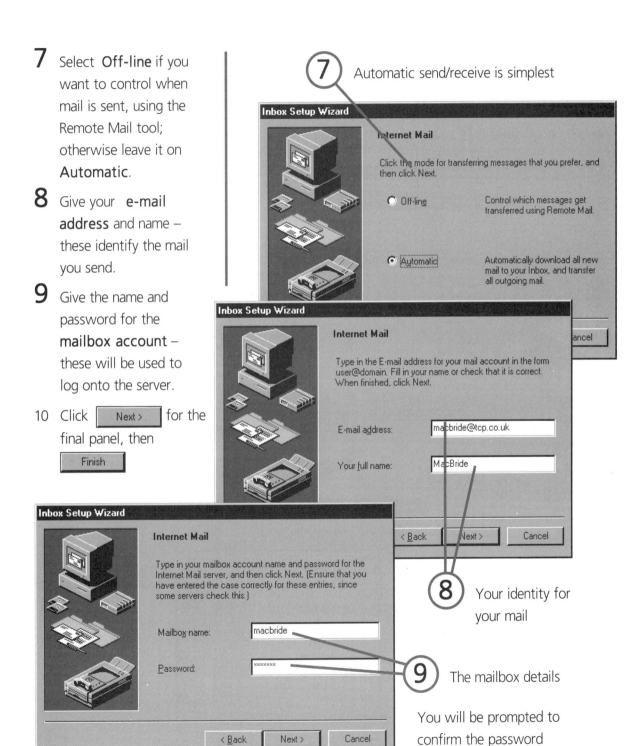

⑦ Automatic send/receive is simplest

Inbox Setup Wizard

Internet Mail

Click the mode for transferring messages that you prefer, and then click Next.

○ Off-line — Control which messages get transferred using Remote Mail.

⦿ Automatic — Automatically download all new mail to your Inbox, and transfer all outgoing mail.

Cancel

Inbox Setup Wizard

Internet Mail

Type in the E-mail address for your mail account in the form user@domain. Fill in your name or check that it is correct. When finished, click Next.

E-mail address: macbride@tcp.co.uk

Your full name: MacBride

< Back   Next >   Cancel

⑧ Your identity for your mail

Inbox Setup Wizard

Internet Mail

Type in your mailbox account name and password for the Internet Mail server, and then click Next. (Ensure that you have entered the case correctly for these entries, since some servers check this.)

Mailbox name: macbride

Password: xxxxxxxx

< Back   Next >   Cancel

⑨ The mailbox details

You will be prompted to confirm the password

Creating a post office

You only need one post office on a small LAN or for each workgroup on a larger network. It should be created on a computer that is on whenever the network is active.

One person should take responsibility for the post office.

Basic steps

1 Open the **Control Panel** and click 🖳 the **Post Office** icon.

2 Select **Create a new...**

3 **Browse** for a drive or folder where the new post office folder can be created.

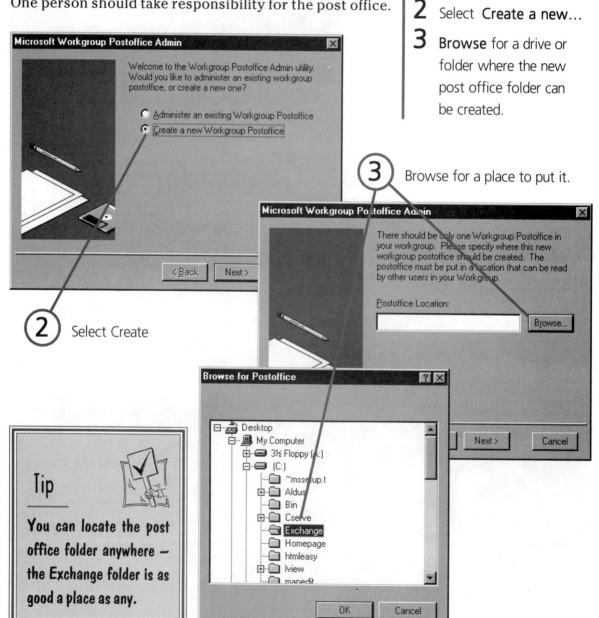

Microsoft Workgroup Postoffice Admin

Welcome to the Workgroup Postoffice Admin utility. Would you like to administer an existing workgroup postoffice, or create a new one?

○ Administer an existing Workgroup Postoffice
◉ Create a new Workgroup Postoffice

< Back | Next >

③ Browse for a place to put it.

② Select Create

Microsoft Workgroup Postoffice Admin

There should be only one Workgroup Postoffice in your workgroup. Please specify where this new workgroup postoffice should be created. The postoffice must be put in a location that can be read by other users in your Workgroup.

Postoffice Location:

Browse...

Next > | Cancel

Browse for Postoffice

- Desktop
  - My Computer
    - 3½ Floppy (A:)
    - (C:)
      - ~mssetup.t
      - Aldus
      - Bin
      - Cserve
      - **Exchange**
      - Homepage
      - htmleasy
      - Iview
      - mapedit

OK | Cancel

Tip

You can locate the post office folder anywhere — the Exchange folder is as good a place as any.

4 Confirm the location.

5 Give details of the post office's **Administrator**.

6 Use **Explorer** to find the folder and open its **Properties** panel.

7 **Share** the post office folder, giving it a meaningful name.

8 Select **Full Access** – set a **Password** only if needed.

The new folder name will start 'wgpo..'

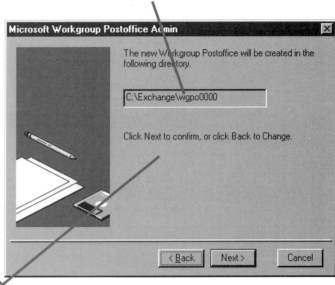

④ Check the location

⑥ Open Properties

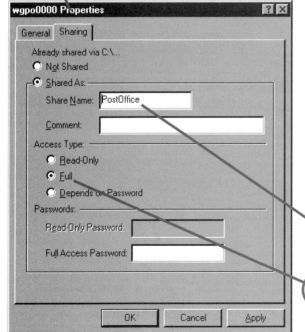

⑤ Give the Administrator's details

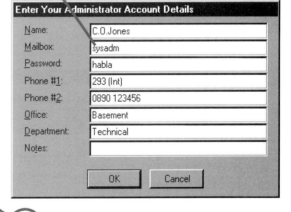

⑦ Share with a recognisable name

⑧ Allow Full access

Adding the users

The post office's manager must set up all user accounts. As part of this, passwords will be assigned to each mailbox. If required, the users can change their passwords from within Exchange.

Basic steps

1 Open the **Control Panel** and click  the **Post Office** icon.

2 Select **Administer.**

3 **Browse** for the post office folder.

4 Enter your **Name** (as post office Manager) and **Password** .

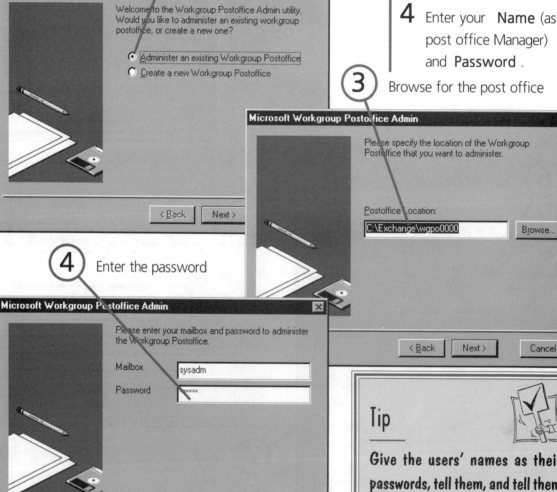

② Select Administer

Browse for the post office

④ Enter the password

Tip

Give the users' names as their passwords, tell them, and tell them how to change the passwords for something more secure

52

5 At the **Post Office Manager** panel click Add User...

6 Fill in the **Name**, **Mailbox** and **Password**, and others as required.

7 Click OK

8 Repeat steps 5 to 7 for all users then click Close

❑ **Changing passwords** (performed by users)

1 Run **Exchange**

2 From the **Tools** menu select **Mail Tools – Change Mailbox Password**.

3 Give the **Old** and **New** passwords.

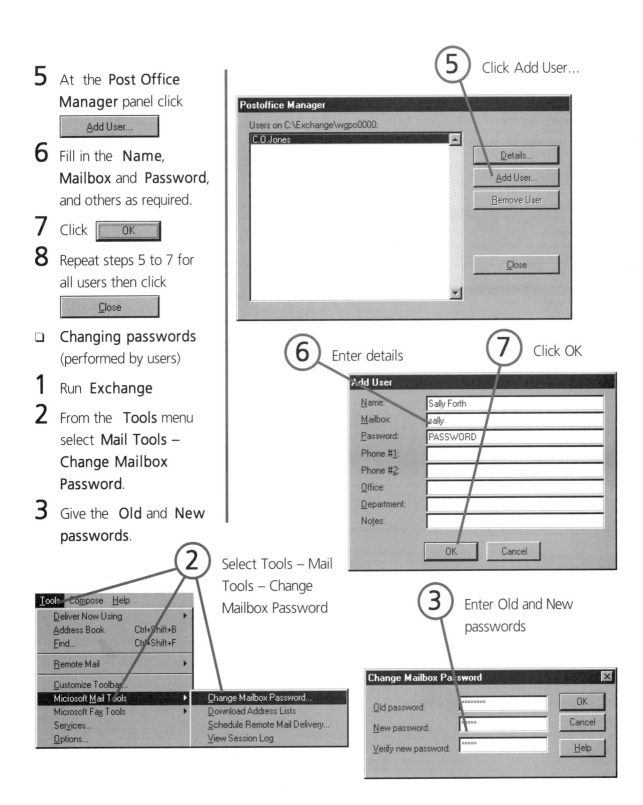

⑤ Click Add User...

Postoffice Manager

Users on C:\Exchange\wgpo0000:

C.O.Jones

Details...
Add User...
Remove User

Close

⑥ Enter details

⑦ Click OK

Add User

Name: Sally Forth
Mailbox: sally
Password: PASSWORD
Phone #1:
Phone #2:
Office:
Department:
Notes:

OK   Cancel

② Select Tools – Mail Tools – Change Mailbox Password

Tools Compose Help
Deliver Now Using
Address Book   Ctrl+Shift+B
Find...   Ctrl+Shift+F
Remote Mail
Customize Toolbar...
Microsoft Mail Tools   ► Change Mailbox Password...
Microsoft Fax Tools   ► Download Address Lists
Services...   Schedule Remote Mail Delivery...
Options...   View Session Log

③ Enter Old and New passwords

Change Mailbox Password

Old password: ********   OK
New password: ****   Cancel
Verify new password: *****   Help

53

Configuring your mailbox

After the post office and the mailboxes have been created, the mail settings on each user's computer should be configured. As the system has taken care of most of the tricky bits, the routine is pretty straightforward.

Select the Mail service

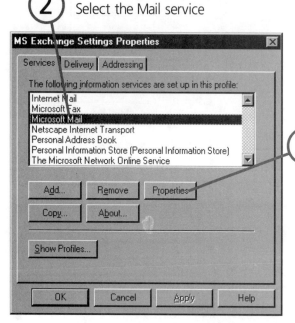

Click Properties

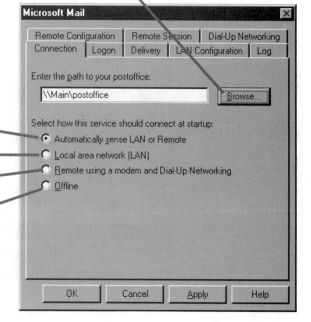

Browse for the post office

Set the connect mode

Use where a modem and network connections are present

For LAN-only mail

For non-networked users

Allows user to control when mail is sent/received, through Exchange's Remote Mail tool.

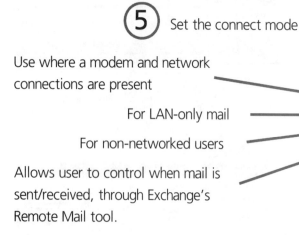

54

6 On the **Logon** tab, enter your **Name** and **Password** if they are not already there.

7 Tick the **automatically enter password** box, if wanted.

8 On the **Delivery** tab, set the **Check mail** interval.

9 On the **Log** tab, tick the **Maintain a session log** box – this can help in tracking errors.

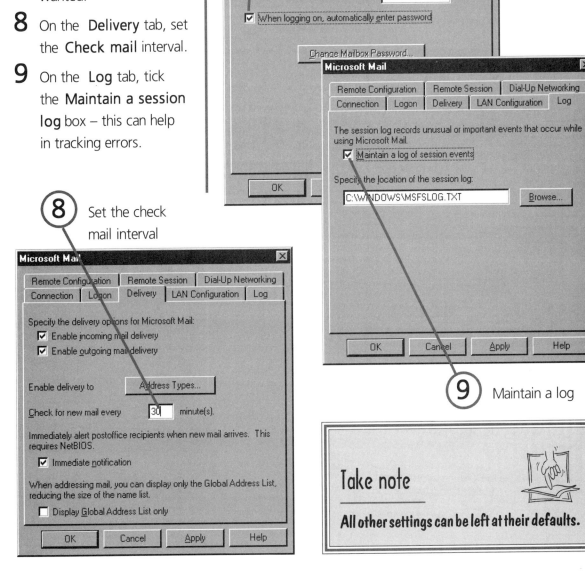

⑦ Automatic password entry?

⑥ Check the name and password

Microsoft Mail

Remote Configuration | Remote Session | Dial-Up Networking
Connection | Logon | Delivery | LAN Configuration | Log

Enter the name of your mailbox: `sally`

Enter your mailbox password: `*****`

☑ When logging on, automatically enter password

Change Mailbox Password...

OK

Microsoft Mail

Remote Configuration | Remote Session | Dial-Up Networking
Connection | Logon | Delivery | LAN Configuration | Log

The session log records unusual or important events that occur while using Microsoft Mail.

☑ Maintain a log of session events

Specify the location of the session log:

`C:\WINDOWS\MSFSLOG.TXT`   Browse...

OK | Cancel | Apply | Help

⑨ Maintain a log

⑧ Set the check mail interval

Microsoft Mail

Remote Configuration | Remote Session | Dial-Up Networking
Connection | Logon | Delivery | LAN Configuration | Log

Specify the delivery options for Microsoft Mail:
☑ Enable incoming mail delivery
☑ Enable outgoing mail delivery

Enable delivery to   Address Types...

Check for new mail every `30` minute(s).

Immediately alert postoffice recipients when new mail arrives. This requires NetBIOS.
☑ Immediate notification

When addressing mail, you can display only the Global Address List, reducing the size of the name list.
☐ Display Global Address List only

OK | Cancel | Apply | Help

Take note

All other settings can be left at their defaults.

55

Dial-Up Networking

If you want to use a service provider other than MSN and have not installed Dial-up networking, open the Control Panel and use Add/Remove Programs to do so now.

There are two aspects to configuring a new connection:

● the network software within your computer

● the connection to the service provider.

Basic steps

1 Open the **Control Panel** and select **Network**

2 Click **Add**

3 Select **Protocol** and click **Add**

4 Select **Microsoft** and **TCP/IP**, then click **OK**

5 Select the TCP/IP entry, click **Properties**

6 Work through the tabs

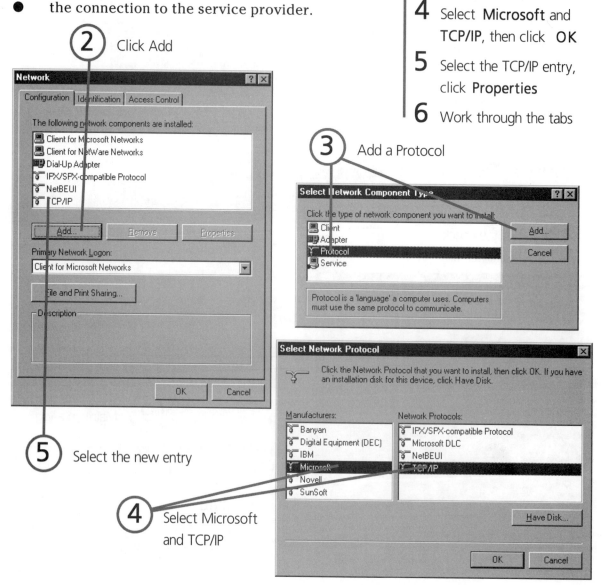

② Click Add

③ Add a Protocol

⑤ Select the new entry

④ Select Microsoft and TCP/IP

IP address: select *Obtain IP address automatically*

WINS Configuration: select *Disable WINS resolution*

Advanced: select *Set this protocol as default*

Bindings: check *Client for Microsoft networks*

Configuration A

Gateway: leave it blank

DNS Configuration: select *Disable DNS*

Configuration B

Gateway: type in the address

DNS Configuration: type your e-mail name as the *Host*, your provider's name as the *Domain*, and ADD their IP address as the *Primary DNS*

Windows 95 is new, and service providers are still adapting to it. I've come across two approaches – one specifies the servers at this point, the other does it in the Dial-Up configuration. Either way you must know your provider's DNS addresses.

(6) Work through the tabs

(A) Disable DNS and leave Gateway blank

(B) Enter DNS and Gateway details

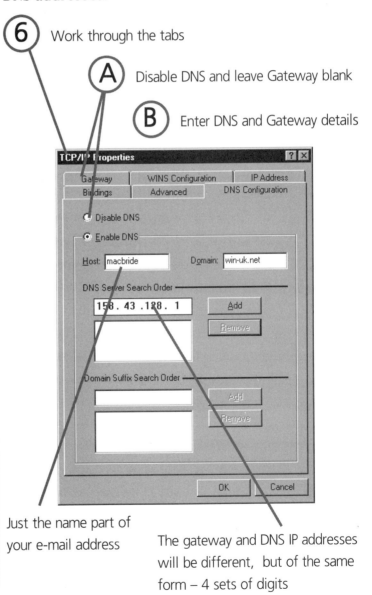

Just the name part of your e-mail address

The gateway and DNS IP addresses will be different, but of the same form – 4 sets of digits

The Dial-Up connection

Once the Network software is in place, you can set up the connection. A Wizard handles the donkey work, leaving it to you to set the Properties.

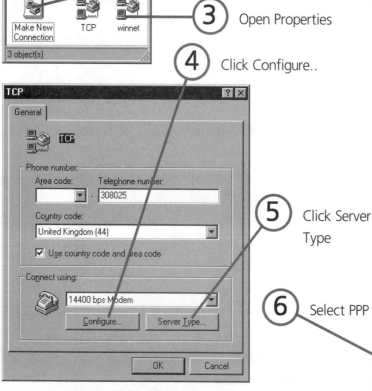

① Make a new connection

③ Open Properties

④ Click Configure..

⑤ Click Server Type

⑥ Select PPP

⑦ Check these Options

Basic steps

1 Open the **Dial-Up** folder and click **Make New Connection**

2 In the **Wizard** enter a name and the phone details

3 Select the connection and open **Properties**

4 Click **Configure** and on the **Options** select *Bring up terminal window after dialling*

5 Click **Server Type**

6 For the **Type**, select *PPP:Windows 95..*

7 Check *Log on* , *Enable compression* and *TCP/IP*

8 Click **TCP/IP Settings**

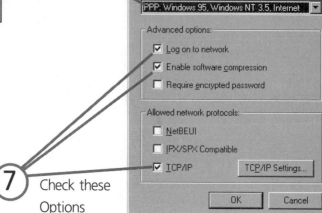

Take note

This configuration won't log you in automatically – people are still looking for a simple way to do that!

58

9 Set **Server assigned IP address**

A WIth Configuration A set **Specify name server** and enter the addresses

B With configuration B set **Server assigned name server address**

❏ **Logging in**

1 Double click the connection's icon

2 Click **Connect**

3 At the Terminal Screen, enter your *user name*, *password* and *PPP* when prompted.

4 After the *Packet mode enabled* (and some garbage), click **Continue**

❏ Run your applications

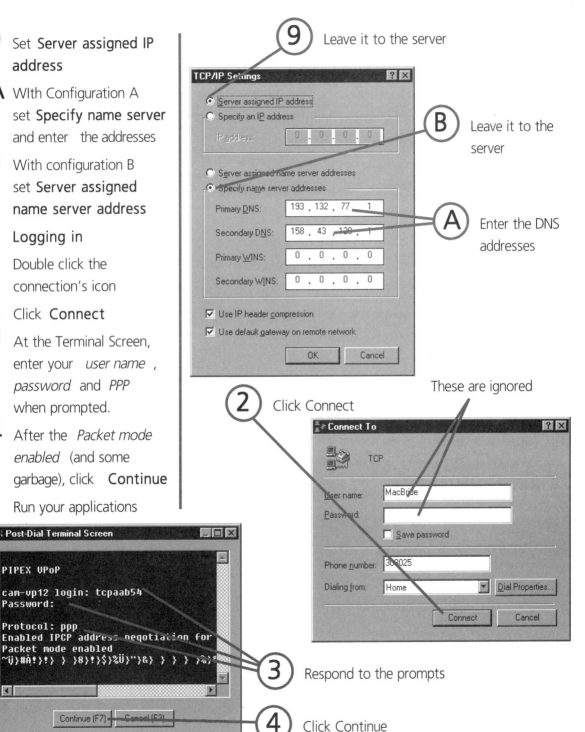

⑨ Leave it to the server

Ⓑ Leave it to the server

Ⓐ Enter the DNS addresses

These are ignored

② Click Connect

③ Respond to the prompts

④ Click Continue

59

Summary

- You can use Microsoft Exchange to communicate within the LAN and by fax and e-mail with the outside world.

- The Inbox Setup Wizard greatly simplifies the business of configuring your system.

- For Internet communications, you must have a modem attached to your computer. There is special software that can share a modem over a LAN, but nothing built into Windows 95 to handle this.

- Before anyone can send mail over the LAN, you must create a post office in a shared folder.

- The post office administrator creates the users' accounts and their initial passwords – these can be changed later by the users.

- Mail settings can be configured to suit individual tastes.

- To use an Internet service provider other than MSN, you must install and configure the Dial-Up Networking software.

5 Microsoft Exchange

Exchange views

Exchange comes equipped with four folders – Inbox, Outbox, Deleted and Sent Items. Messages are stored in the appropriate folder as they are composed, received, deleted and posted. Opening the Folders pane is the key adustment you should make to the display.

There are also several other options that you can set to make Exchange easier to use.

● Use the Columns panel to decide what information to show about each message;

● Use Customise Toolbar to add or remove icons from the Toolbar.

Basic steps

❑ **The Folders pane**

1 Click [📧] or open the **View** menu and turn on **Folders**.

2 Adjust the position of the dividing line between the panes to suit yourself.

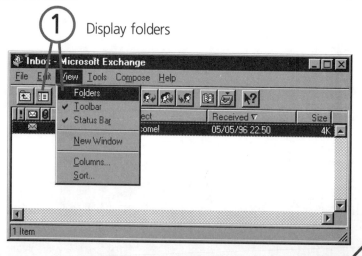

Display folders

Adjust the layout

Tip

You can create new folders – e.g. for long-term sorted storage of mail – and move items between them.

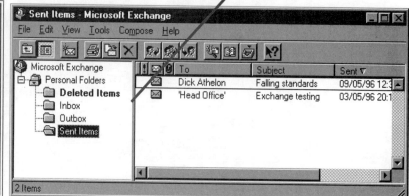

Basic steps

❏ **Columns**

1 Open the **View** menu and select **Columns**

❏ **To add an item**

2 Select the item from the **Available** list and click ` Add -> `

3 Shuffle the item into place with ` Move Up ` and ` Move Down `

❏ **To remove an item**

4 Select the item from the **Show the following** list and click ` <- Remove `

❏ **Toolbars**

1 From the **Tools** menu select **Customize Toolbars...**

2 Continue as above, using Separators to divide the icons into sets.

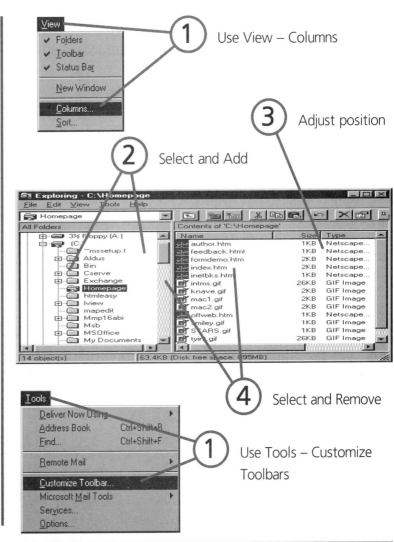

① Use View – Columns

③ Adjust position

② Select and Add

④ Select and Remove

① Use Tools – Customize Toolbars

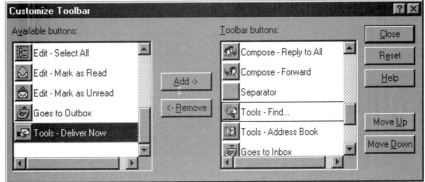

Incoming mail

E-mail is easy to send, virtually cost-free within a network and very cheap over the Internet. As a result, you may well find that you get rather more of it than you do of ordinary (smail) mail – and the volume will no doubt increase as more and more people get on-line. It is important to learn how to deal with incoming mail efficiently!

Messages can, of course, be read. They can also be:

● *ignored*, if the From name and Subject entries show they are of no interest – you get some junk e-mail over the Internet, apart from anything else;

● *replied to*, with the option to send the reply to all the people who would have received copies of the message;

● *forwarded* to a third party, with comments attached;

● *deleted* when they have been dealt with.

Basic steps

1 Click on the **Inbox** folder to open it.

2 Check the **From** and **Subject** entries to see what's there.

3 Select the message and click ☒ to remove unwanted mail.

Take note

When you delete messages, they are moved to the Deleted folder. Delete from there to remove them from the system.

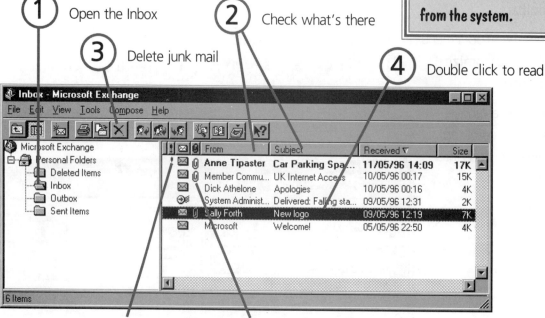

① Open the Inbox

③ Delete junk mail

② Check what's there

④ Double click to read

Important   FIle attached

4 Double click on a message, or select it and press **[Enter]** to open it for reading.

5 Reply or forward, if wanted. Note that the text of the message is copied in, though attached files are only shown as a name.

6 Click ⊠ to return to the Inbox window.

Delete

Reply to sender

Reply to all who received it

Forward to someone else

⑥ Close

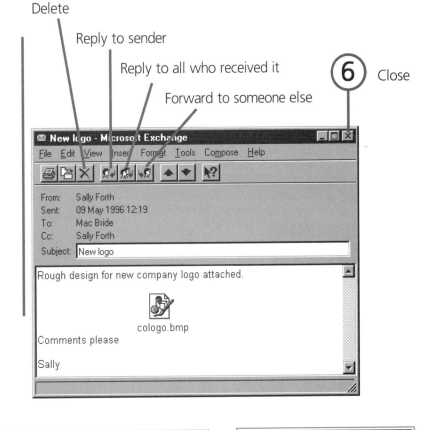

⑤ Add your comments and reply?

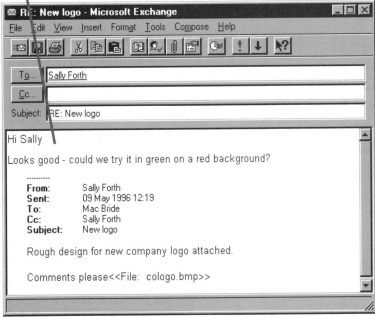

Tip

If you want to reply to, or forward, a message, you can do it either from the message window or the main Exchange window.

65

Sending a message

Sending a message is easy – if you have the address. That presents no problem for other people on your network, as their addresses are at hand. Finding e-mail addresses for external contacts can be trickier. We will come back to those in Section 7.

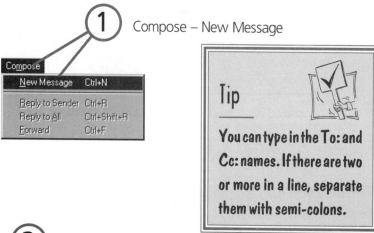

① Compose – New Message

② Click for the Address Book

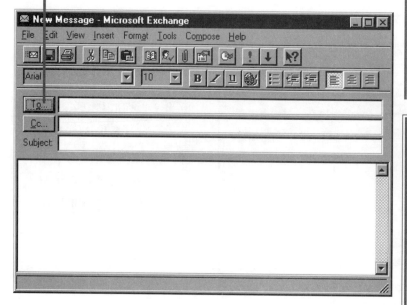

Basic steps

1 Click or open the **Compose** menu and select **New Message**.

2 Click `To...` to open the **Address Book**.

3 Select a name from the list and click `To ->`.

4 To send copies, select the name(s) and click `Cc ->`

5 Click `OK`

6 Type in a **Subject** line.

7 Type your message.

8 Set the importance and properties as required – see page 68.

9 Click or open the **File** menu and select **Send** to post the mail.

Tip

You can type in the To: and Cc: names. If there are two or more in a line, separate them with semi-colons.

Take note

You can have any number of To: and Cc: names. Use To: if you want people to reply to the mail; Cc: when copies are sent for information only.

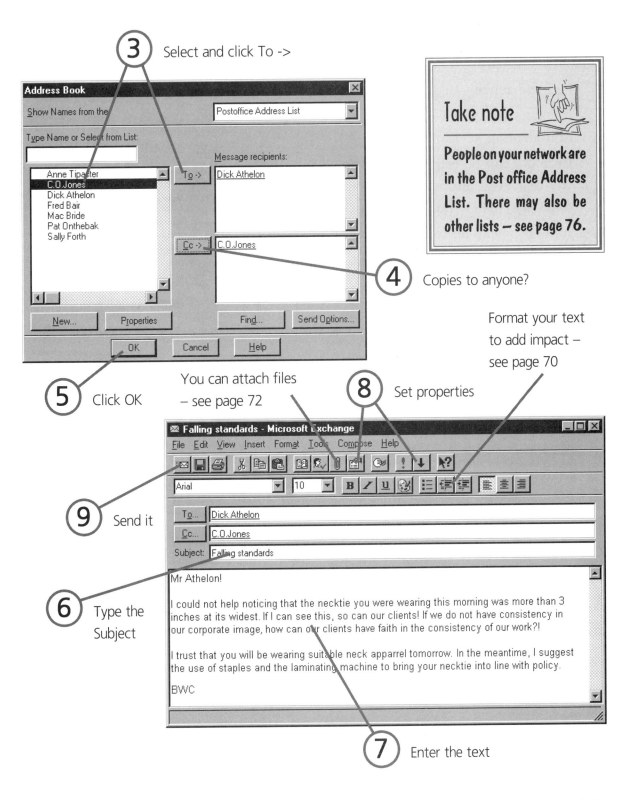

③ Select and click To ->

Address Book ☒

Show Names from the: [Postoffice Address List ▼]

Type Name or Select from List:

```
Anne Tipaster
C.O.Jones
Dick Athelon
Fred Bair
Mac Bride
Pat Onthebak
Sally Forth
```

[To ->]

Message recipients:

Dick Athelon

[Cc ->] C.O.Jones

[New...] [Properties] [Find...] [Send Options...]

[OK] [Cancel] [Help]

People on your network are in the Post office Address List. There may also be other lists – see page 76.

Take note

④ Copies to anyone?

Format your text to add impact – see page 70

⑤ Click OK

You can attach files – see page 72

⑧ Set properties

☒ Falling standards - Microsoft Exchange

File Edit View Insert Format Tools Compose Help

Arial ▼ 10 ▼ **B** _I_ U

⑨ Send it

To... Dick Athelon
Cc... C.O.Jones
Subject: Falling standards

⑥ Type the Subject

Mr Athelon!

I could not help noticing that the necktie you were wearing this morning was more than 3 inches at its widest. If I can see this, so can our clients! If we do not have consistency in our corporate image, how can our clients have faith in the consistency of our work?!

I trust that you will be wearing suitable neck apparrel tomorrow. In the meantime, I suggest the use of staples and the laminating machine to bring your necktie into line with policy.

BWC

⑦ Enter the text

67

Message properties

You can set the properties of outgoing mail in four ways:

● Its **importance** – High, Normal or Low.

● Its **sensitivity** – Normal, Private, Personal or Confidential.

● **Receipts** can be requested to show when the mail was delivered, and when it was read (the latter only applies to mail within the network.)

● A file copy can be kept in the **Sent Items** folder.

These properties can be set as defaults and reset for individual messages.

❑ **Setting defaults**

1 Open the **Tools** menu and select **Options.**

2 Switch to the **Send** tab.

3 Tick the boxes if **receipts** are wanted

4 Open the **Sensitivity** list and set the level.

5 Set the default **Importance** level.

6 Tick the **Save** box if file copies are wanted.

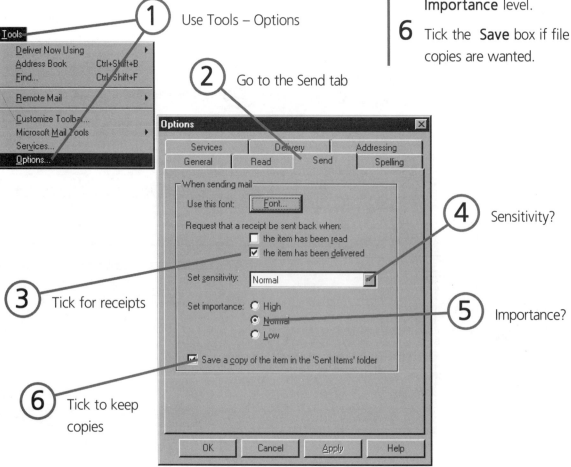

① Use Tools – Options

② Go to the Send tab

④ Sensitivity?

③ Tick for receipts

⑤ Importance?

⑥ Tick to keep copies

Basic steps

❑ **Single messages**

1 Click ![High] to set High or ![Low] Low importance

2 Click ![receipt] to request a read receipt

or

3 Click ![properties] or open the **File** menu and select **Properties**.

4 Set the **Sensitivity, Importance, Receipt** and **Save** options as required.

5 Click **OK**

Tip

Leave the Sensitivity and Importance levels at normal until you have seen how you are using the mail, then set them to suit the majority of your messages.

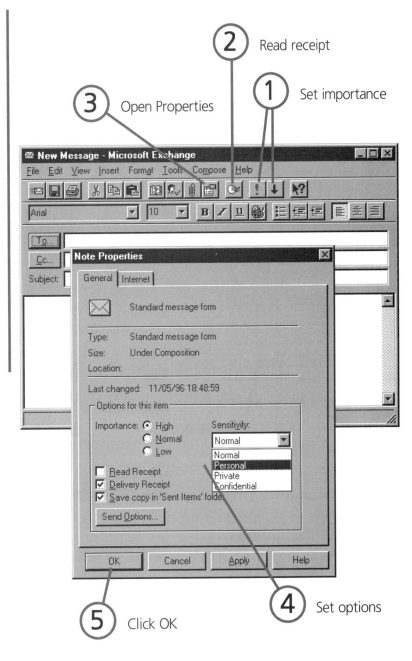

② Read receipt

③ Open Properties

① Set importance

④ Set options

⑤ Click OK

69

Formatted mail

One of the advantages Exchange has over most e-mail systems is that you can format the text, using colours, fonts, sizes or styles to pick out points in your messages.

Use the Formatting Toolbar to set individual aspects, and the Font and Paragraph panels for more complex styling.

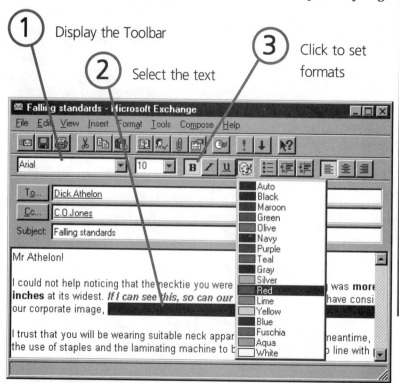

① Display the Toolbar

② Select the text

③ Click to set formats

Basic steps

1 Turn on the **Formatting Toolbar** from the **View** menu.

2 Select the text to be formatted.

Either

3 Click an icon to toggle a style on, or drop down the Font, Size or Colour lists

or

4 Open the **Format** menu and select **Font** or **Paragraph**.

You can set several aspects of the text at the same time in the panels.

The Formatting Toolbar

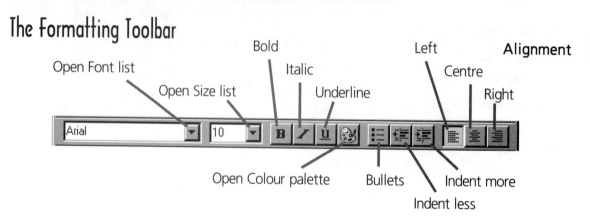

Open Font list

Open Size list

Bold

Italic

Underline

Open Colour palette

Bullets

Indent less

Indent more

Left

Centre

Right

Alignment

70

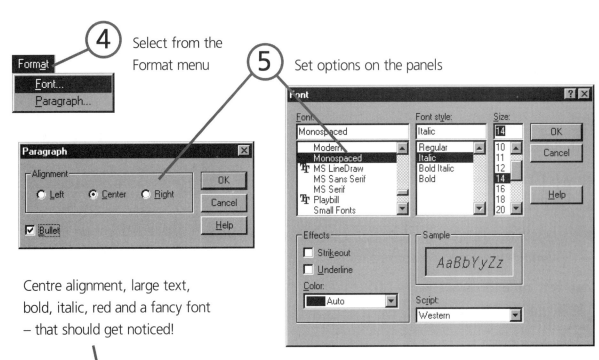

④ Select from the Format menu

⑤ Set options on the panels

Centre alignment, large text,
bold, italic, red and a fancy font
– that should get noticed!

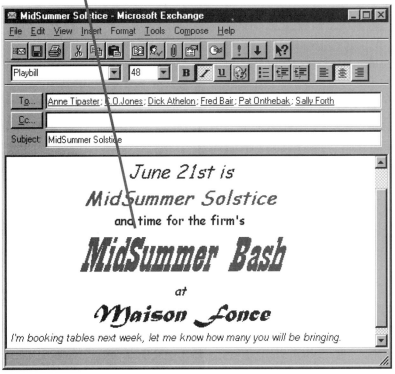

Tip

Don't waste your time setting formats that your readers can't see. Not everyone will have your fonts, and readers outside the network may be using other – plain text – e-mail systems.

Attaching files

If you use Microsoft Word or Write, you will probably be used to inserting graphics and other objects into your text. Exchange offers the same facilities, with the additional option to insert message within messages.

You can insert existing files or create new ones from within Exchange.

An inserted **file** can be placed:

● As an *attachment*, the file is sent within the message.

● As a *link*, the message only has a shortcut to the file – which must be in a shared folder .

Inserted **objects** are always attachments, but can be displayed in full or as icons.

Basic steps

❑ Inserting files

1 Move to the place in your text where the object is to fit.

2 Open the **Insert** menu and select **File**.

3 Locate the file – find it through **Network Neighborhood** if you want to link it.

4 Tick **Link** if the file is available in a shared folder on.

5 Click [OK]

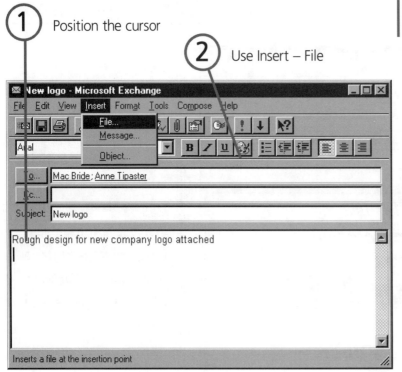

① Position the cursor

② Use Insert – File

Take note

If you link an inserted file from a folder on your own machine, you must enter the full path across the network to the file. (See page 74.)

72

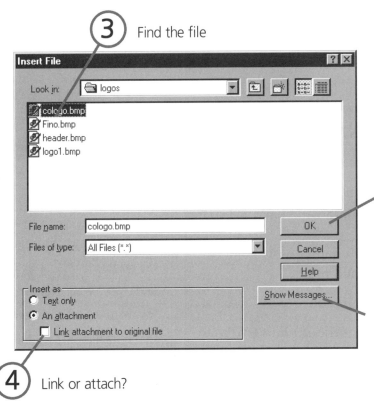

③ Find the file

⑤ Click OK

④ Link or attach?

Switches to the **Insert Message** dialog, where you can select a message from your Exchange folders. That dialog similarly has a **Show Files** button to switch to the **Insert File** dialog.

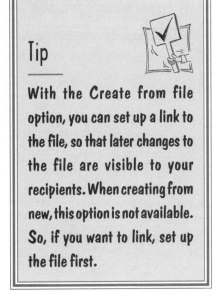

Tip

With the **Create from file** option, you can set up a link to the file, so that later changes to the file are visible to your recipients. When creating from new, this option is not available. So, if you want to link, set up the file first.

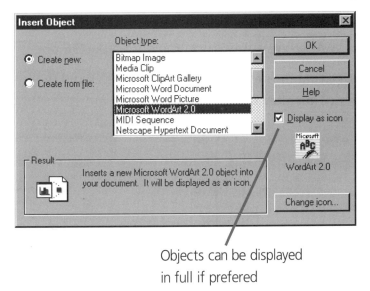

Objects can be displayed in full if prefered

Network paths

When setting up a link to a file across the network – as in Exchange's Insert File routine – you must give the *network* path to that file. This is not quite as obvious as it sounds.

Suppose that you wanted to link the file 'REPORT96.DOC' from the Winword folder on your C: drive, and that your computer was named as 'ACCOUNTS' on the network.

There are two routes you can take to reach it.

● Start from My Computer and travel down through the C: (or other drive). The path will be of the type:

Drive:\Folder\Folder...

In the example, the path would read:

C:\MSOffice\Winword\report96.doc

● Start from Network Neighbourhood, move first to your machine – *on the network* – then down through its drives and folders. The path takes the form:

\\MachineName\Drive\Folder\Folder...

In the example, the path would read:

\\Accounts\C\MSOffice\Winword\report96.doc

Notice that the network path starts with \\ and that there is no colon after the drive letter.

Take note

When selecting a file from the Insert File dialog, you must start from Network Neighborhood if you want the system to create the right path for you. If you select the file from your local drive, you will have to type in the path yourself.

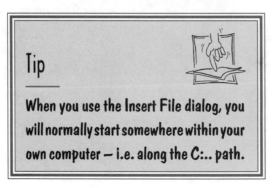

Tip

When you use the Insert File dialog, you will normally start somewhere within your own computer – i.e. along the C:.. path.

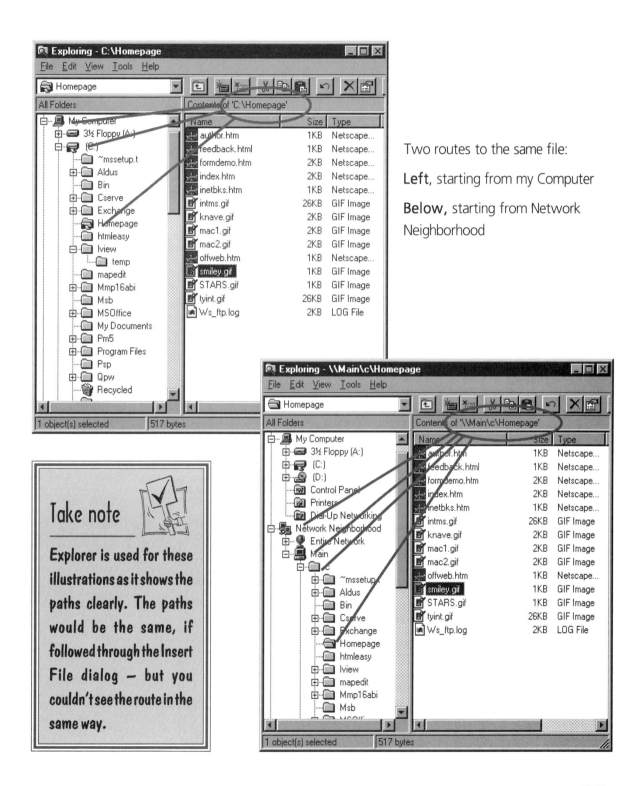

Two routes to the same file:

Left, starting from my Computer

Below, starting from Network Neighborhood

Take note

Explorer is used for these illustrations as it shows the paths clearly. The paths would be the same, if followed through the Insert File dialog — but you couldn't see the route in the same way.

Address book

If you are just sending message across the local network, you don't have to think too much about the Address Book – the users and their e-mail addresses are all there for you.

The Address Book comes into its own when you start to send e-mail beyond the local network. We won't, in fact, be covering this until Section 6, but let's look at the Address Book now before we leave Exchange.

An Address Book can contain a number of lists, including:

● **Personal Address Book** – your own set of contacts (the subject of the next few pages);

● **Postoffice Address List** – the users on your system;

● **Microsoft Network** – an on-line directory of members (only avalaible if you belong to MSN.)

Basic steps

1 Click [📖] or open the **Tools** menu and select **Address Book**.

2 Drop down the **Show Names from the:** list and select **Personal Address Book**.

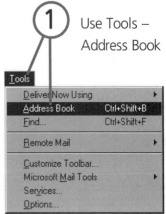

① Use Tools – Address Book

New entry   Properties of selected entry

Find   Add to Personal Address Book

Delete   New message to selected contact

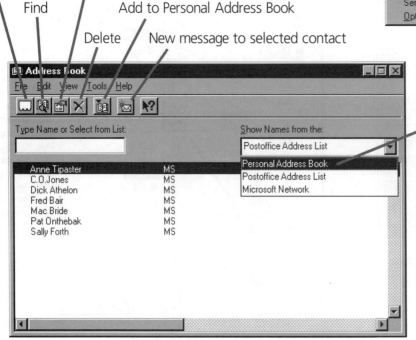

② Select a list

76

Basic steps

Adding a new entry

❏ **MSN members**

1 Click 🖳 or open the **File** menu and select **New Entry...**.

2 Select **Internet over the Microsoft Network**.

3 For the **E-mail address**, type in the name – the part up to @.

4 Type the remainder of the address in the **Domain name** slot.

5 Enter the contact's real name into **Name**.

The way that Internet e-mail address are written is slightly different for MSN users than for those who have accounts with other service providers.

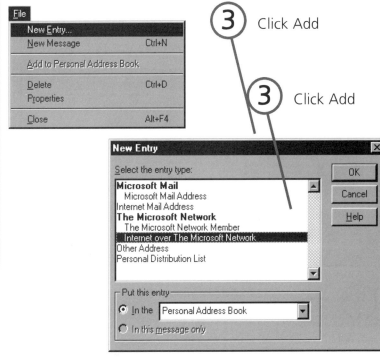

③ Click Add

③ Click Add

③ Click Add

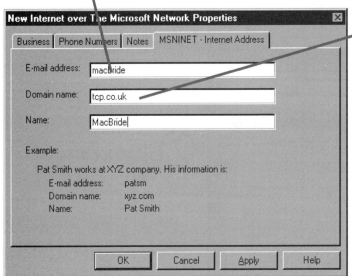

③ Click Add

One of my e-mail addresses is:

macbride@tcp.co.uk

Here it is, split at the @ sign into **E-mail address** and **Domain name** for the Internet over MSN panel.

③ Type the contact's name

④ Enter the full e-mail address

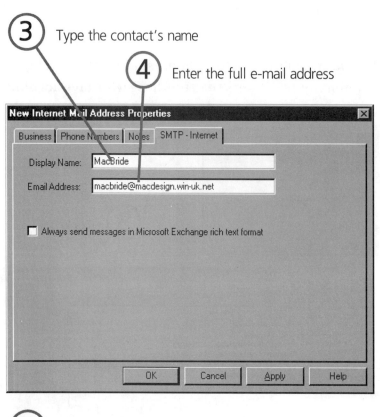

❏ **Non-MSN users**

1 Click ⬜ or open the **File** menu and select **New Entry....**

2 Select **Internet Mail Address**.

3 Give a recognisable **Display name**.

4 For the **E-mail Address**, type in the whole address, as it is normally written.

❏ **Editing entries**

5 Locate the entry in the names list.

6 Right click for the short menu, or open the **File** menu.

7 Select **Properties**.

⑤ Locate the entry

⑥ Right click for the menu

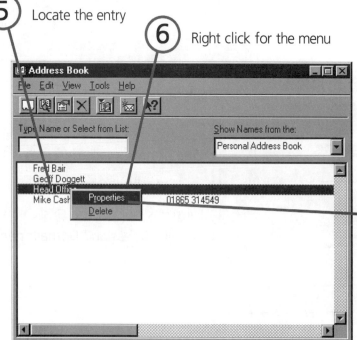

⑦ Open the Properties panel

78

Basic steps

❑ **Setting the numbers**

1 Open the **Address Book** and switch to the **Phone Numbers** tab.

2 Type in the numbers for your contacts.

❑ **Dialing out**

3 Make sure the modem is plugged in and turned on.

4 Click [Dial...]. The **Dialing** dialog appears, closely followed by the **Call Status** display.

5 When you hear the ringing tone, click [Talk] – don't wait for the person to pick up the phone as it will screech at them!

Phone numbers

You can do more than just store phone numbers in Exchange. If you have a modem, you can use the Exchange to dial the stored numbers for you.

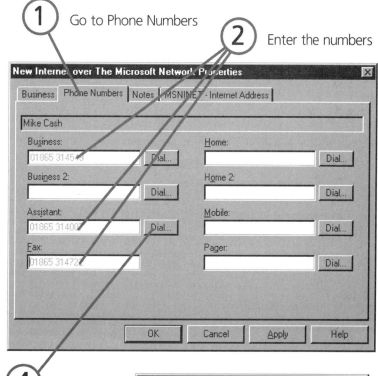

① Go to Phone Numbers

② Enter the numbers

④ Click Dial

⑤ Click Talk

Putting the receiver down also closes the conection.

Summary

❑ You can adjust the Exchange window to suit yourself. The most important adjustment is to turn on the Folders display.

Incoming mail can be replied to, forward to a third party, deleted or ignored – as well as read! .

To send a message, you first define who it is being sent to and who gets copies, then type in a Subject and your message.

You can set the importance and sensitivity of outgoing mail, and request that receipts be sent to you when it is delivered and when it is read.

Where a message is being sent to another Exchange user, you can enhance the text with formatting. This serves no purpose where the recipient has a plain-text mail reader.

Files can be attached to messages as inserted objects. Within the LAN they can also be attached as links to files in shared folders.

When linking a file to a message, you must give the full network path.

The Address book has at least two sections: the Post office address list holds address of the LAN's users; your Personal Address Book is mainly intended for external e-mail addresses.

You can store contacts' phone numbers in Exchange, and dial them from your computer if it has a modem attached to it.

6 Schedule+

Starting up

Schedule+ can be used as a personal organiser, but if you are on a local or extended network it can also be used for arranging meetings of group members. It has three main elements:

● A list of **Contact** names, addresses, phone and fax numbers, with a handy built-in phone dialler.

● A **Planner**/appointments calendar, with a reminder facility.

● A **Things To Do** list, for scheduling tasks and monitoring their progress.

The three elements can be interrelated, linking tasks to contacts or meetings, and contacts to meetings.

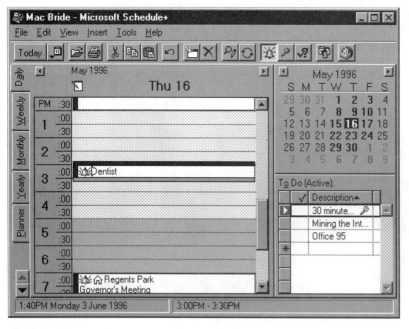

You can choose which view to use
– see page 85

All three elements can be viewed in a variety of ways. For example, the calendar can be displayed on a yearly, monthly, weekly or daily basis. The example here has a multiple view, showing the day, the month and the current To Do list.

Basic steps

Initial set-up

- ❏ **The Schedule file**

1 At start up, turn on the **Group- enabled mode**.

2 Select **Create a new schedule file**.

3 At the **Save** dialog box type your name and click ⌐ Save ⌐.

The first couple of times that you use Schedule+, there will be some little chores to do.

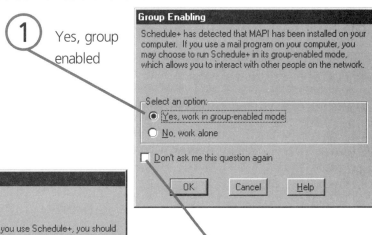

① Yes, group enabled

If you always work the same way, set the mode then click here

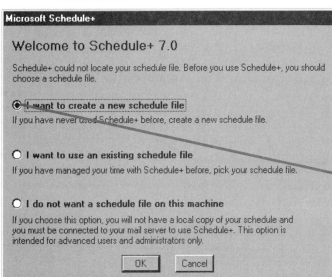

② Select create new

③ Type a name and Save

On subsequent start-ups, Schedule links to your post office account, to handle the mail.

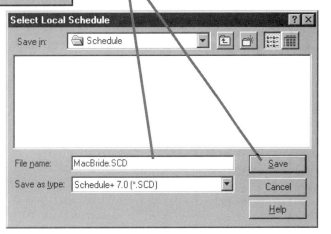

The Schedule+ tools

With most Windows software, it is often easier at first to work from the menus, as they show you clearly what your choices are. Schedule+ is no exception. The menus are well-organised and very comprehensive. The View commands, for instance (see right), give you a high degree of control over the display.

All the regularly used commands are also present on the toolbar. Note that *Recurring event*, *Reminder*, *Private* and *Tentative date* are all toggles – click once to set, click again to clear.

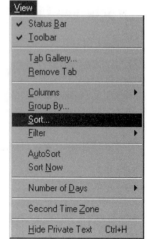

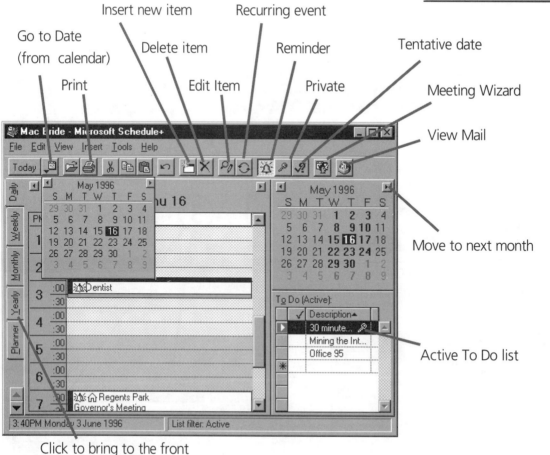

Insert new item

Go to Date
(from calendar)

Print

Delete item

Edit Item

Recurring event

Reminder

Private

Tentative date

Meeting Wizard

View Mail

Move to next month

Active To Do list

Click to bring to the front

Basic steps

1 Open the **View** menu and select **Tab Gallery**

❑ **Adding a tab**

2 Select a tab from the left pane, using the **Preview** and **Description** to get an idea of its display

3 Click [**Add ->**]

4 Move it up or down as necessary

❑ **Removing a tab**

5 Select a tab from the right pane

6 Click [**<- Remove**]

Tip

An unwanted tab can be removed from the main display. Select it and use View – Remove Tab.

The Preview is small, but useful. The Description can be incomprehensible if you don't know the jargon

Tabs and views

The default set up has tabs for Daily, Weekly and Monthly diaries, the Planner, To Do list and Contacts. Tabs can be added or removed, to suit your way of working, using the option on the View menu.

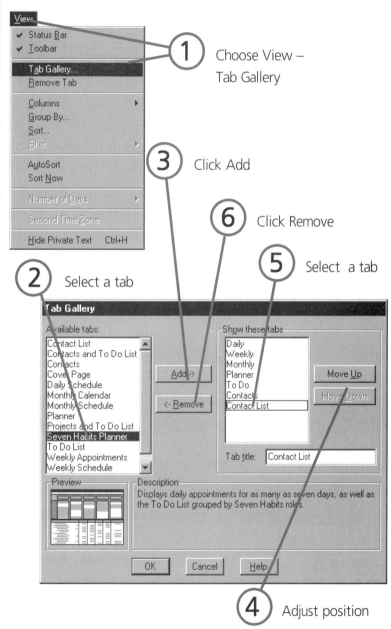

Choose View – Tab Gallery

Click Add

Click Remove

Select a tab

Select a tab

Adjust position

The Contacts list

This is probably the most straightforward part of Schedule to set up. Mind you, it will take a while if you give all the details that it can hold – home and business address, phone and fax, birthdays, spouse, assistant, dog's name....

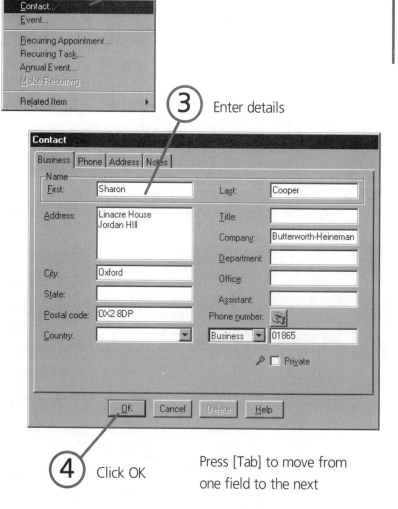

② Use Insert – Contact

③ Enter details

④ Click OK

Press [Tab] to move from one field to the next

Tip

When you are first adding contacts, you can enter the details in the main list display, but they will not put themselves in order. Use View – Sort to reorganise the list.

Basic steps

Phone dialling

1 Open the **Contacts** tab

2 Type the first letter(s) of the last name into the **Go to** slot to focus the list.

3 Select the person

4 Open the **Phone** tab

5 Click 📞 beside the number you want

6 Lift the phone

7 When the number rings, click ‾‾Talk‾‾

You can dial out from Schedule+, just as you can from Exchange's Address Book.

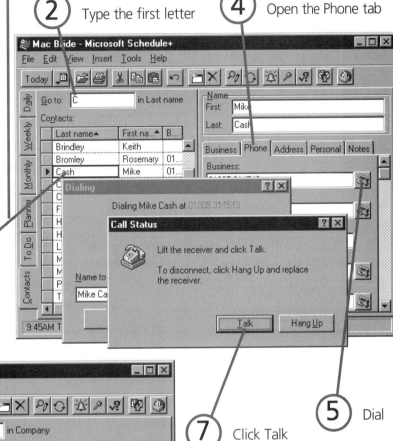

② Type the first letter

④ Open the Phone tab

③ Select the contact

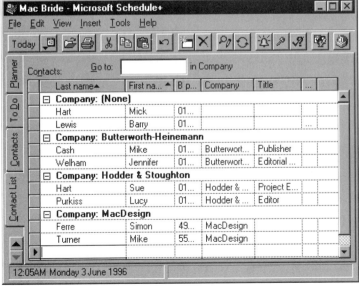

⑦ Click Talk

⑤ Dial

Tip

The Contacts list can be sorted by Company if you give the necessary details.

Making a date

Appointments are at the heart of Schedule+, and there are a number of optional refinements here.

① Open a date tab ② Go to the day

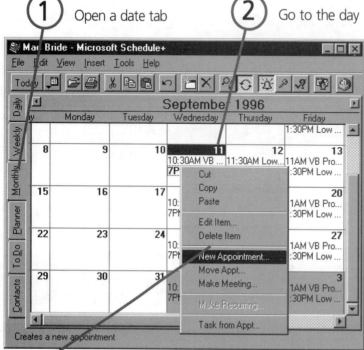

③ Right click and select New Appointment

④ Set the times

⑤ Enter a Description

⑦ Click OK

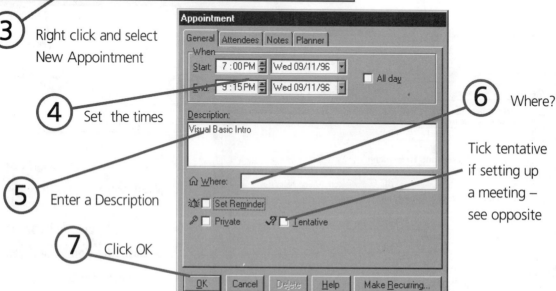

⑥ Where?

Tick tentative
if setting up
a meeting –
see opposite

1 Open the **Daily**, **Weekly** or **Monthly** tab

2 Move to the day of the appointment

3 Right click to open the short menu and select **New Appointment**

4 Type the **Start** and **End** times, or highlight the hours/minutes and click the little arrows

5 Enter a **Description**

6 Enter the **Where** location if relevant

7 If you are not setting options, click **OK**

88

Basic steps

1 Set up a (tentative) appointment as shown opposite.

2 Switch to **Attendees**.

Either

3 Type the names of **Required** or **Optional** attendees or who will supply **Resources**.

or

4 Click ⬚Invite Others...⬚ and select names from the Post office List, or your Personal Address Book.

Arranging meetings

Schedule+ makes it very simple to arrange meetings with other people on your LAN – as long as they all keep their own Schedule+ diaries up to date! It can also be a convenient way of calling a meeting with those that you can contact by fax or e-mail.

③ Add names   ② Open the Attendees tab

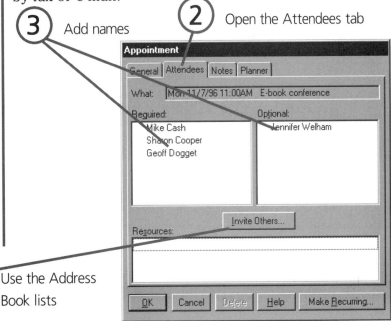

④ Use the Address Book lists

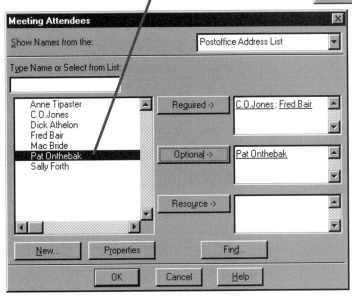

Take note

If you are typing names, they must match those in your Exchange Address Book.

Open the Planner tab

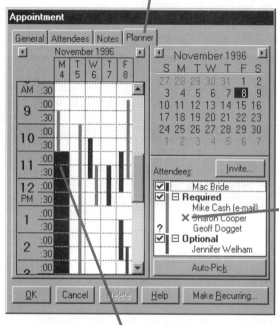

To retime the meeting, point to
the new start and drag the
highlight to the end time

Check for clashes

5   Open the **Planner** tab.

6   Check for clashes – you
    can only do this for
    those whose Schedules
    are on your network.

7   When the details are
    set, click [OK   ].
    The **Meeting Request**
    panel opens.

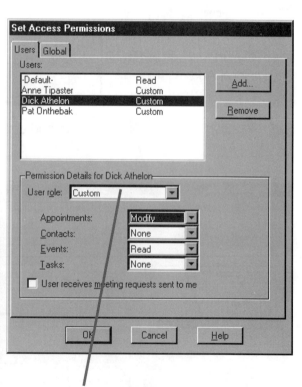

With the Custom option, you
can set specific permissions
for the selected user.

Tip

**To simplify planning internal meetings, get your
network users to allow others to check their
diaries. Tools – Set Access Permissions opens
this panel. Permissions can be set for all
(default) or for named users, Added to the list.
Read access lets others see, but not change,
data in a Schedule file. None keeps data private.**

Basic steps

8 The **To** (Required), **Cc** (Optional) and **Subject** (Description) lines will have been filled in. To send copies to other people, write their names in the Cc slot, separating them with semi-colons

9 Type a brief note to let people know about the meeting

10 Click 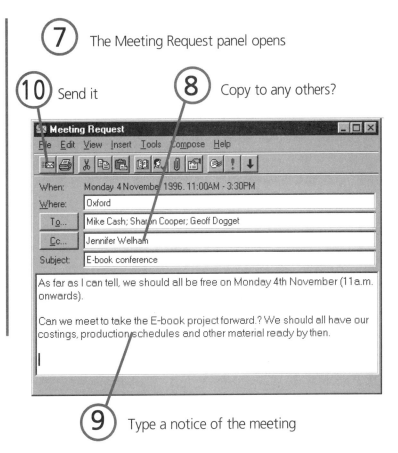 to send the e-mail

⑦ The Meeting Request panel opens

⑩ Send it

⑧ Copy to any others?

Meeting Request _ □ ×

File   Edit   View   Insert   Tools   Compose   Help

When:	Monday 4 November 1996. 11:00AM - 3:30PM
Where:	Oxford
To...	Mike Cash; Sharon Cooper; Geoff Dogget
Cc...	Jennifer Welham
Subject:	E-book conference

As far as I can tell, we should all be free on Monday 4th November (11a.m. onwards).

Can we meet to take the E-book project forward.? We should all have our costings, production schedules and other material ready by then.

⑨ Type a notice of the meeting

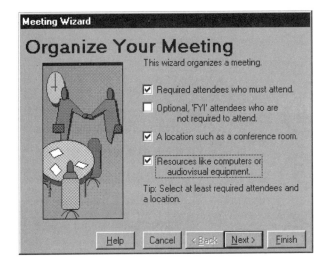

Meeting Wizard

Organize Your Meeting

This wizard organizes a meeting.

☑ Required attendees who must attend.

☐ Optional, 'FYI' attendees who are not required to attend.

☑ A location such as a conference room.

☑ Resources like computers or audiovisual equipment.

Tip: Select at least required attendees and a location.

Help   Cancel   < Back   Next >   Finish

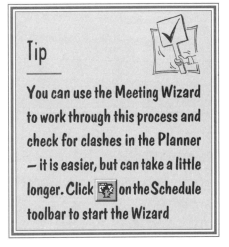

Tip

You can use the Meeting Wizard to work through this process and check for clashes in the Planner — it is easier, but can take a little longer. Click [icon] on the Schedule toolbar to start the Wizard

Tasks from appointments

It is often the case that you need to do preparatory work for an appointment or meeting. This can easily be logged in your Schedule by creating a task from the appointment.

1 Open a date tab and select the appointment

2 Right click and choose **Task from Appt....**

3 The **Ends** date will have been set up, but you need to set the **Starts before**

4 Edit the **Description** to show what needs doing

5 Set the **Reminder** time if wanted – and turn it off, if not

6 Click **OK**

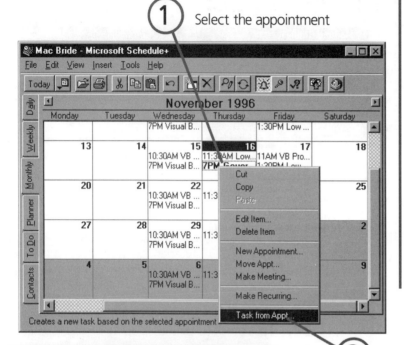

① Select the appointment

② Pick Task from Appt..

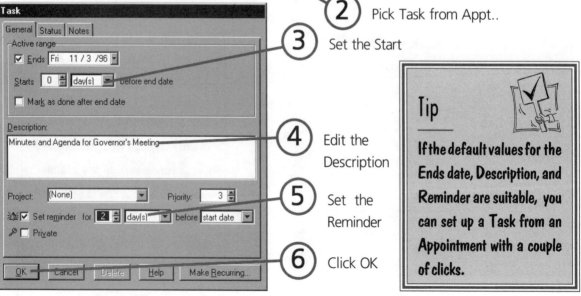

③ Set the Start

④ Edit the Description

⑤ Set the Reminder

⑥ Click OK

Tip

If the default values for the Ends date, Description, and Reminder are suitable, you can set up a Task from an Appointment with a couple of clicks.

Basic steps

The To Do list display

❑ **Filtering**

1 Open the **View** menu and point to **Filter**

2 Select the type to display

❑ **Sorting and Grouping**

3 Open the **View** menu and select **Sort.. (or Group..)**

4 Select the first criterion from the list

5 Set the direction – **Ascending** or **Descending**

6 Repeat for the next two levels of sort (or group), if wanted.

If you are a very busy person, or are just not too good at finishing things off, your To Do list could get crowded. Make the display easier to read, either with a Filter (based on completion status) or by Grouping and Sorting to focus on key tasks.

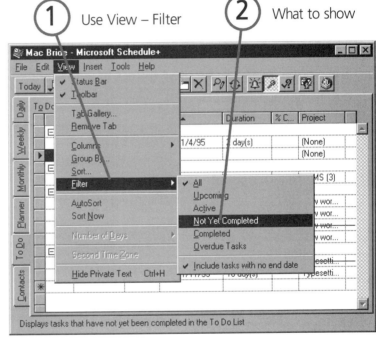

① Use View – Filter

② What to show

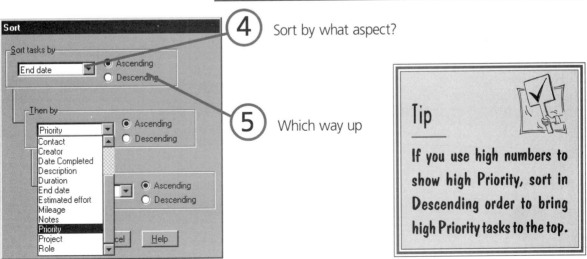

④ Sort by what aspect?

⑤ Which way up

Tip

If you use high numbers to show high Priority, sort in Descending order to bring high Priority tasks to the top.

Summary

❑ Schedule+ is a **personal** and **workgroup organizer** in which you can store contacts, appointments and lists of tasks.

❑ When **first starting up** you will need to specify a filename for your Schedule+ data.

❑ Schedule+ can be run in **single-user** or **group** mode.

❑ You can select the **Tabs** to be included in your display.

❑ The **Contacts list** can be used to record very complete details of your contacts.

❑ You can **dial phone numbers** in your Contacts list by clicking the dialler button.

❑ When adding **appointments**, you can set them to **recur** weekly, monthly or at any fixed interval.

❑ **Reminders** can be set for any time before an appointment.

❑ People in networked groups can arrange **meetings** through Schedule+. The Meeting Wizard can handle the donkey work for you.

❑ The **To Do list** can be used to schedule activities and to record progress on them. Reminders can be set for time-limited tasks.

7 MSN

The Microsoft Network

At the time of writing, the Microsoft Network has been going for only a few months but has already made a significant impact. It provides a good range of worldwide services, with special interest areas for the UK, Germany, France, Japan and the USA. Internet e-mail has been there from the start, and full Web-browsing, newsgroup reading and file transfer access to the Internet is now in place. By the time you read this, local dial-in access should be available throughout the UK.

Setting up MSN is very largely automatic. Once you have started the process, the software takes over, prompted you for a little information from time to time, but otherwise managing very well by itself. The programs on your distribution disk are probably out of date, but MSN will recognise this and organise an update, on-line.

☐ Setting up

1 Use **Add/Remove Programs** to install the Microsoft network software.

2 Run **SIGNUP.EXE** in the **Microsoft Network** folder.

3 Follow the prompts. It will enroll you, then offer to download and install updates to the software – take up the offer as it improves the system.

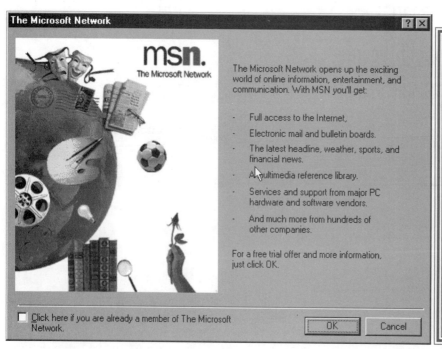

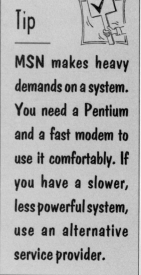

Tip

MSN makes heavy demands on a system. You need a Pentium and a fast modem to use it comfortably. If you have a slower, less powerful system, use an alternative service provider.

Basic steps

Logging in

1 Double click  the MSN icon.

2 Enter your **Member ID** and **Password**.

3 Check the **Remember** box.

4 Click Settings... .

5 On the **Connection Settings** panel, click Access Numbers .

During the registration process, you will have selected a user name for yourself and been allocated a password. The first time that you log in, you will need to enter these into the main panel. If you tick the *Remember my password* box, logging in will be simpler next time.

● Check the Settings before that first log in.

② Enter your details

③ Tick Remember

④ Click Settings

⑤ Click Access Numbers

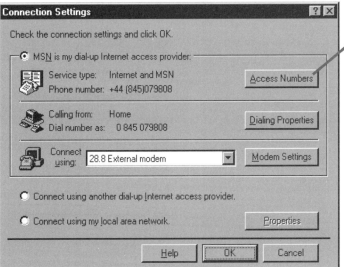

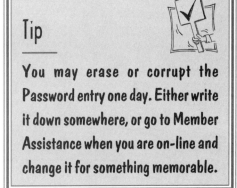

Tip

You may erase or corrupt the Password entry one day. Either write it down somewhere, or go to Member Assistance when you are on-line and change it for something memorable.

Basic steps

6 Select a Service type

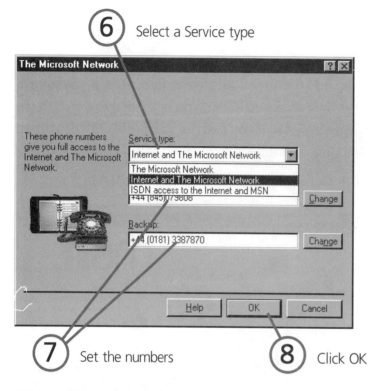

7 Set the numbers **8** Click OK

Bring up the windows if you have trouble getting on-line. When you ring for technical support, you can tell them what you see.

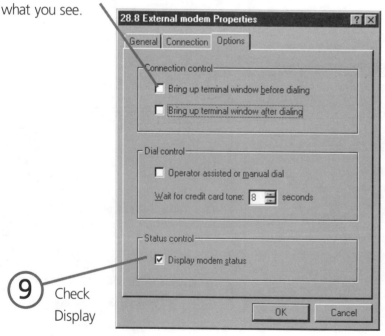

9 Check Display

6 Select a **Service type,** specifying *Internet* if you want to go Web-browsing through the MSN connection.

7 Click Change and pick the closest **Primary** and **Backup** numbers.

8 Click OK to return to the main panel, then click Modem Settings

9 Check the **Display modem status box** if you have an internal or hidden modem.

Take note

The modem status display (on the right of the status bar) has 'lights' that flash green when data is flowing. If they stick on red when you are trying to download, you know that you have lost the connection. This happens from time to time.

MSN Today

When you sign in to MSN, two panels appear – MSN's main control panel (see next page) and MSN Today. This brings into one place the most used facilities – e-mail, internet centre, favourite places, the members' directory and help – plus a selection of the newest additions to the service.

In a way, it typifies the MSN approach. It's easy to use, constantly updated, well-designed and highly graphical. If you have a fast modem and a good local connection to MSN, the service is a pleasure to use.

"What's on" changes almost every day

You can explore the Internet from here

Add places to your list as you find them

Categories

MSN's services are organised into *categories*. Categories act much like folders, and the display looks and is used like that of My Computer, though the contents will be more varied. Categories may contain:

- Other categories, sub-divided by topic or country.

- Shareware, freeware, demos and other files.

- Reference works and information services, some run by MSN, others by specialist businesses.

- Forums (a special type of category) where people can share their interests and expertise.

- Bulletin boards (BBS) where people can post articles, questions – and answers.

- Chat rooms, where you can real-time (typed) conversations with other members.

Basic steps

1 At the MSN or MSN Today panel, click Categories.

2 At each level of category, either click on a folder icon to open a sub-category

or

3 Click on another icon to access a service.

4 To set up a quick link to a category or service, open the **File** menu and select **Add to Favorite Places**.

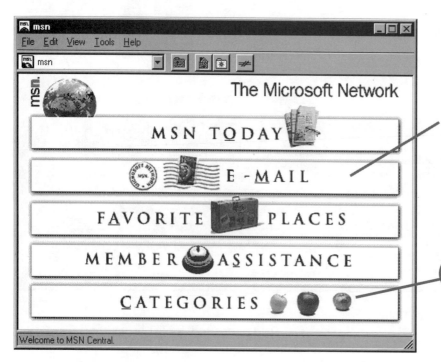

Click E-mail to run Exchange and pick up or send your messages – see page 104

(1) Click Categories

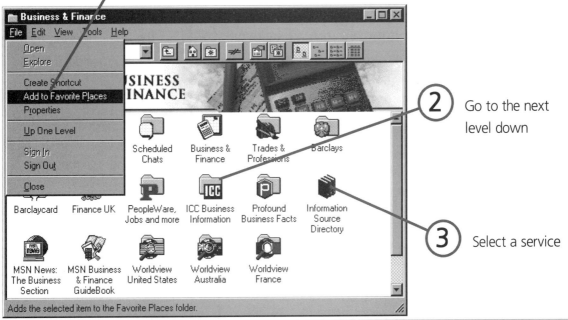

④ Add to Favorite Places?

② Go to the next level down

③ Select a service

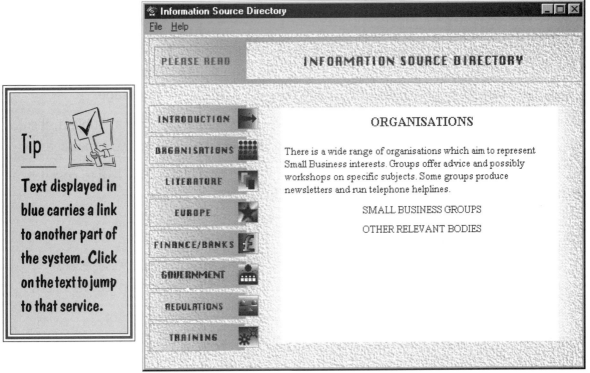

Tip

Text displayed in blue carries a link to another part of the system. Click on the text to jump to that service.

Bulletin Boards

The BBSs (Bulletin Board Services) can be a effective way to make contact with others who share your profession or interest. They are also a good source of answers to questions – particularly on computer-related matters.

(1) Find an interesting BBS

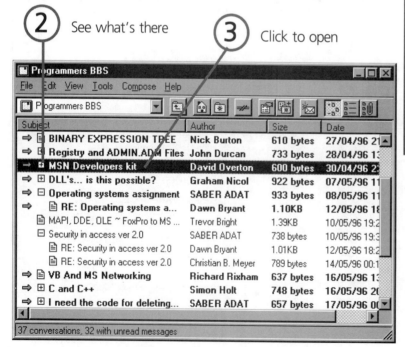

(2) See what's there

(3) Click to open

1 Go to **Categories** and work down through the levels, looking for folders marked *BBS*.

❑ **Reading articles**

2 Scroll through the list of articles, clicking ⊞ to show all the messages in a set.

3 Click on a message to read it.

4 Use the controls in the viewer to move to nearby articles.

❑ **Posting an article**

5 From the **Compose** menu, select **New Message**.

6 Enter a **Subject**, then type your message.

7 Click 🖂 to post it.

Related messages are grouped in 'conversations'.

④ Read nearby articles

Messages

Next

Previous   Next unread

Conversations

Previous   Next

Next unread

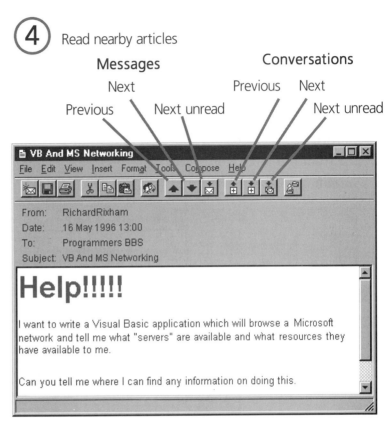

⑦ Post it

⑥ Type the Subject and message

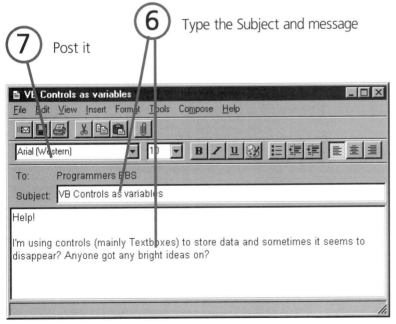

External e-mail

For the most part, sending e-mail to people in MSN or in the wider Internet is the same as within the LAN. There are a few times when a slightly different approach is needed:

● When composing a message, type in a full Internet address, or select from your Personal Address Book, or from the Microsoft Network – the system will go on-line to access this.

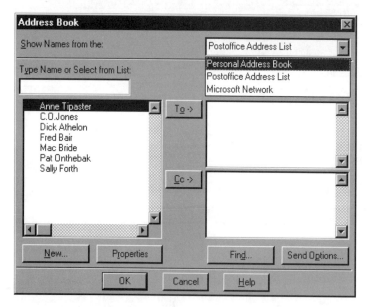

● When you have finished the message, select your service from the Tools – Deliver Now Using... list.

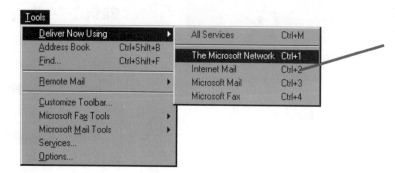

Internet addresses

❏ All Internet addresses take the form:

name @domain.address

e.g.:

gates @microsoft.com

macbride @tcp.co.uk

❏ MSN has a directory of all its members, and it is sometimes possible to find people's e-mail addresses elsewhere on the Internet (see *Internet Resources Made Simple*). In general, the best way to get someone's address is to ring them up and ask for it!

If you have an account with another Internet access provider, the link will be marked Internet Mail in the options.

Basic steps

1
Run **Exchange**.

2
Open the **Tools** menu, select **Remote Mail** then the service.

3
Wait while the system connects to the mail service.

4
Open the **Tools** menu and select **Connect and Update Headers**.

5
Mark the items you .want to read, then select **Connect and Transfer Mail**.

Take note

When you login to MSN normally, the system will automatically check for new messages.

If you compose messages while you are on-line, a simple 'Send' will mail the messages through the service.

Remote mail

The Remote mail facility allows you to login to MSN and check your mailbox, from within Exchange. Once logged in, getting the mail is a two-stage process. First get the headers, with the subject, sender, date, etc. then select those that you want to read and download them.

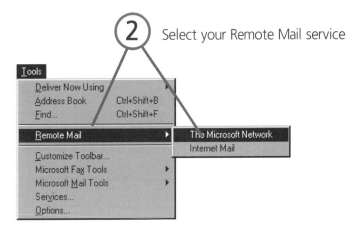

② Select your Remote Mail service

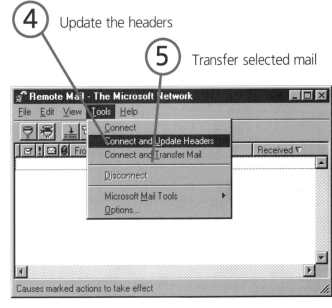

④ Update the headers

⑤ Transfer selected mail

Summary

- ❑ The Microsoft Network offers a good variety of on-line services and can be used for full Internet access.

- ❑ If you set the system to remember your password, logging in is quicker and simpler.

- ❑ The central part of the service is MSN Today. This gives quick access to the most commonly used facilities and alerts you to the latest developments.

- ❑ MSN's services are organised into topic or country-based categories.

- ❑ MSN members can exchange ideas on topics through the many Bulletin Boards

- ❑ The close link between Exchange and MSN's software makes it easy to send and receive external e-mail.

8 Internet Explorer

Internet essentials

These two pages aim to provide an instant guide to the Interent, for those readers who have yet to step into cyberspace.

Computers and connections

The Internet consists of several million computers and computer networks, connected by a combination of fast special-purpose cable and satellite links and the public telephone network. It reaches into almost every country in the World, though its base – and its largest presence – is in the US.

Around 4 million of the computers act as *hosts*, providing services to the Internet's users. Some hosts allow remote users to access their disks of program and data files. Some offer directories and search facilities so that users can easily find files, facts and people. Some allow users to run programs on their computers, or control interactive devices that are attached to them.

Three types of organisations maintain the host computers and pay for the dedicated links between them.

- Universities and government agencies, who provide facilities as an academic and public service.

- Businesses, who use it to market their products and services, offering free facilities to attract the public. An increasing number of these services, particularly advertising, publishing and information retrieval, arisie directly out of the Interent itself.

- Access Providers, who connect firms and individuals – as users – onto the Internet.

Tip

If you need an introduction to the Internet, try "The Internet for Windows 95 Made Simple" or "The Internet Made Simple".

For more on finding facts, files, people and places, see "Internet Resources Made Simple".

URLs

Every file, page and person on the Interent has a Uniform Resource Locator (URL) which tells you what type it is, where it is and what it is called.

The basic form is:

type://site/path/filename

The *type* can be:

http:// Web page

ftp:// file for transferring

news:// newsgroup

gopher:// Gopher file

mailto:// person's address.

Take note

No single organisation owns the Internet. It is a co-operative venture, loosely controlled by agreement between its users — and it works.

The Web and the Net

The **World Wide Web** is only on easpect of the Internet – though the most important one for most people. It is made up of over 20 million pages on computers scattered throughout the world, interwoven by hypertext links between them. It is accessed through a Web browser, such as Internet Explorer, which can display the formatted text and graphics that make up the page.

Each page has an address to identify the computer, folder and file. These addresses can be attached to words or pictures in other pages, creating a hypertext link. Clicking on such a link in a browser makes the download the addressed page.

Other key approaches to the Internet are:

● E-mail – see page 104.

● News groups – an extension of the e-mail system that allow people to share ideas with others who have a comon interest. (Page 126.)

● FTP – File Transfer Protocol – a standard method for copying files over the Internet. Only certain hosts hold databases of files for ftp'ing. Some of these are software firms that offer upgrades, bug-fixes and help for users; others are universities or service providers who hold stocks of shareware.

● Gopher – The Gopher system used to provide the easiest way to find facts and files on the Internet. It has now been very largely replaced by the Web.

Using Internet Explorer

If you use MSN for Interent access, Internet Explorer is the natural – though not the only – choice of Web browser.

Three good reasons for using Explorer:

● It integrates fully with MSN and with Windows 95 – Explorer knows how to display or otherwise deal with any registered File Types (see page 114.)

● Frequently used sites can be accessed quickly. When you visit a page, its text and images are cached on your hard disk. When you return to it, the disk files are used (as long as they haven't changed) instead of downloading the page again.

● The latest version can be downloaded – for free!

And one reason for preferring Netscape.

● Explorer cannot handle pages containing frames and there is an increasing number of such pages.

Take note

There is no essential link between MSN and Explorer. MSN members can equally well use Netscape or any other browser, and Explorer can be used if you connect through another Internet access provider.

The Explorer Toolbar

Go to Start page

Back to previous page

Go to Search page

Forward to next

Read newsgroups

Send mail

Increase/decrease font size

Paste

Print current page   Reload page   Add to Favorites   Copy

Open Location or File   Stop loading   Open Favorites list   Cut

The Toolbar, Address bar and Status bar can all
be turned off to give a larger viewing area.

Address bar shows the URL of the current page

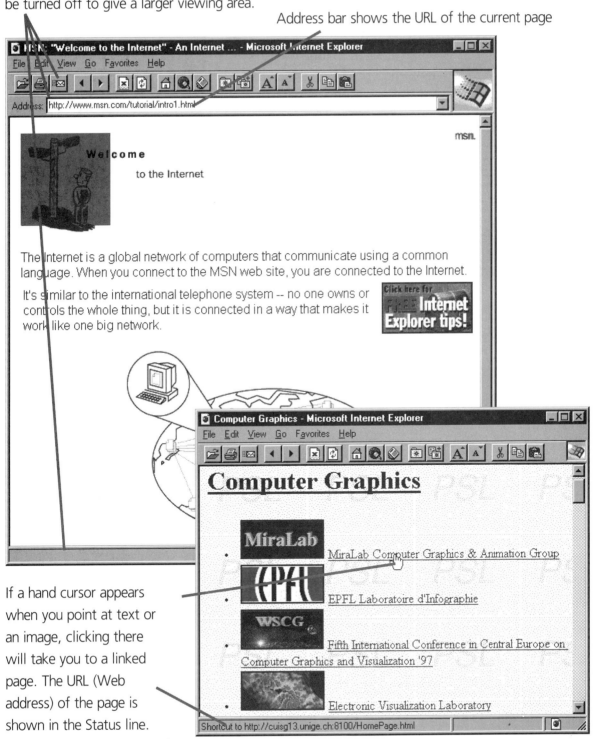

If a hand cursor appears when you point at text or an image, clicking there will take you to a linked page. The URL (Web address) of the page is shown in the Status line.

Options

To get the best out of Explorer, you should set the Options to suit your own way of working. Don't rush into this. Have a few sessions with the default settings first. You will then have a better idea of what settings will work best for you.

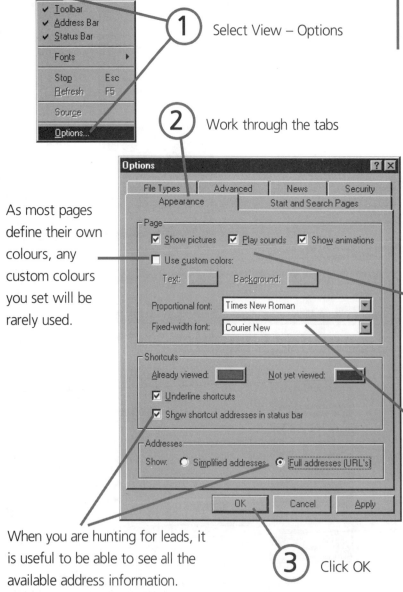

Select View – Options

Work through the tabs

As most pages define their own colours, any custom colours you set will be rarely used.

When you are hunting for leads, it is useful to be able to see all the available address information.

Click OK

1 Open the **View** menu and select **Options...**

2 Work through the tabs, changing the settings as required.

3 Click [OK] to fix the settings

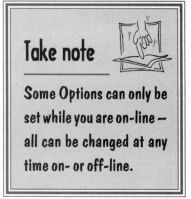

Take note

Some Options can only be set while you are on-line – all can be changed at any time on- or off-line.

Turn *on* the pictures, sounds and animations for attractive Web pages – or *off* for faster working.

Keep the fonts clear and simple – some pages have a poor mix of text/ background colours, and fancy fonts can make them more unreadable.

If you find a page that you would like to go to when you log in – or when you want to search for something – come to this tab and set it as the Start or Search Page by clicking [Use Current]

Security is important – go for the Medium or High options. Click the button to learn more about the security issues.

If you use another service provider – not MSN – you will need to type in your news server address and your e-mail details.

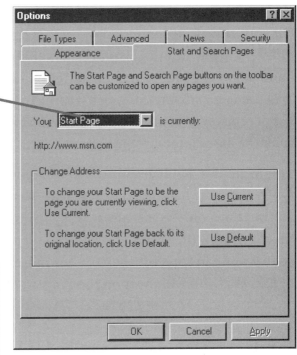

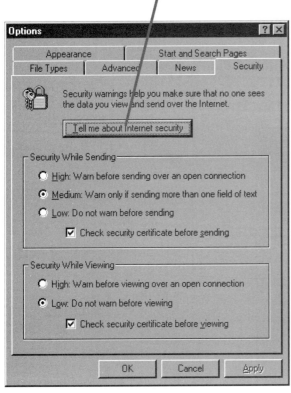

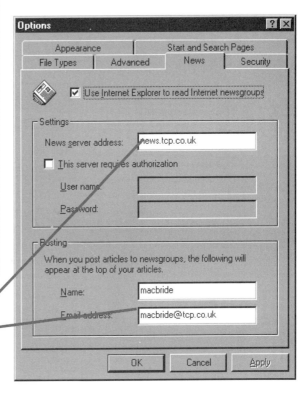

File types

On your travels around the Interent, you will meet many different types of files. Explorer has built-in routines to handle only the most common varieties – such as GIF and JPEG images. For anything else it turns to the Windows 95 list of registered file types. If it finds the type in the list, it runs the associated program to open the file.

The Windows 95 accessories will extend the range of types you can handle, and you may have other useful software on your system already. If you do not have them, there are a few programs that you should get and register, so that you can cope with some of the more common types of files that you will meet on the Web.

Basic steps

1 Run **View – Options** and switch to the **File Types** tab.

2 Look through the list to see if the type is already registered.

3 Click [New Type...]

4 Enter a meaningful **Description**.

5 Enter the file type's **Extention**.

6 Drop down the **Content Type (MIME)** list. Select a suitable type *if available* .

7 Click [New...]

8 Enter " *open* " in the **Action** slot.

9 Click [Browse...] and locate the program.

10 Click [OK] to work back to the **File Types** tab.

11 If the program can handle several types of file, repeat steps 3 to 10 for each extension.

(2) Check the list

(1) Go to File Types

(3) Click New Type

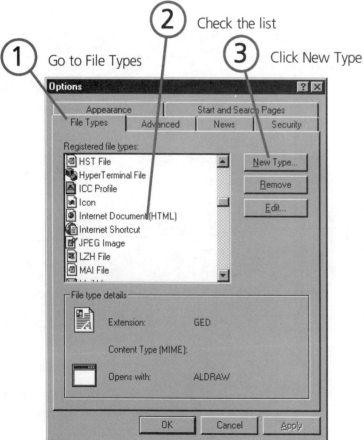

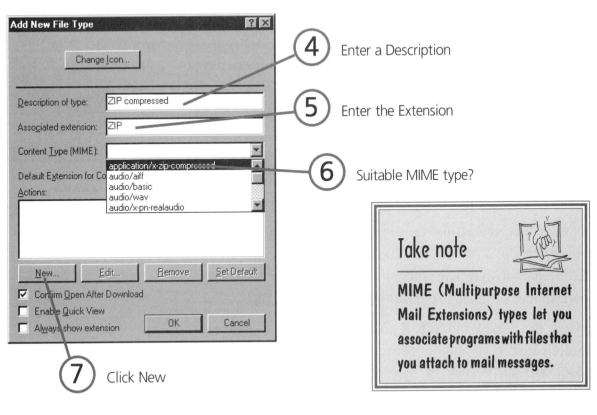

④ Enter a Description

⑤ Enter the Extension

⑥ Suitable MIME type?

⑦ Click New

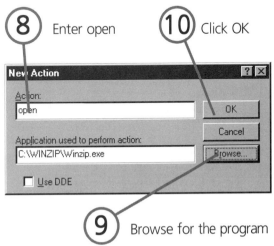

⑧ Enter open

⑩ Click OK

⑨ Browse for the program

Viewers for graphics

If you need an application that can handle a wide range of graphics – not just viewing, but also converting between formats and editing – try Lview Pro or Paint Shop Pro.

Lview Pro

This is the smaller of the two. Lview can read and save graphics in JPG, BMP, DIB, GIF, TGA, PCX, PPN and TIFF formats. This should be enough to cope with the majority of images that you will meet on the Web.

At the time of writing, it was available on the Net as *Lviewp1b.zip*, a 300Kb file. To install it, simply set up a folder and unzip it. The whole lot takes less than 700Kb of disk space, with the program being just over 500Kb.

Lview Pro has a full set of tools for adjusting colour, adding text, cropping, copying, rotating and mirroring. Most are fairly easy to use, and there is a brief but adequate Help system.

JPG and GIF

❑ The **JPG** extension identifies the JPEG (Joint Photographic Experts Group) format. This handles graphics as 256 greyscales or 24-bit colour.

❑ The **GIF** (Graphic Information Format) standard was developed by CompuServe. It is limited to a maximum of 256 colours.

❑ Both have built-in compression, with JPGs being usually, but not always, more compact.

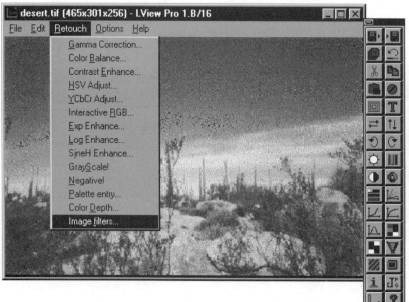

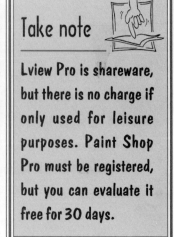

Take note

Lview Pro is shareware, but there is no charge if only used for leisure purposes. Paint Shop Pro must be registered, but you can evaluate it free for 30 days.

Paint Shop Pro

Take note
_____

Both packages can be downloaded from:

ftp://src.doc.ic.ac.uk/ pub/packages/simtel/ win3/graphics

Look for view1b.zip and psp311.zip.

This is a much more substantial package than Lview Pro and capab le of handling just about every graphic format from Word Perfect graphics to Kodak PhotoCD. The latest version (3.0) is on the Net as *psp30.zip* – a 1.3Mb file. This unzips to reveal a SETUP program and a further zipped file. SETUP will install it to its own directory, taking just under 4Mb of space. It is slower to load than Lview, and therefore less suitable for use as a viewer.

On the positive side, Paint Shop Pro has excellent editing facilities and is easy to use. Its approach to filters is a good example of this. Using the Filter Browser, you can preview the effect quickly and clearly before applying a filter. More experienced users can also define their own filters.

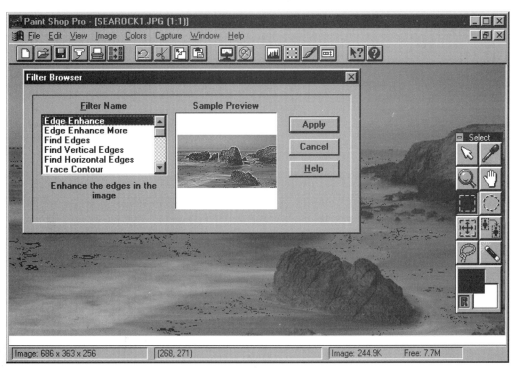

Formatted text

Three types of formatted text files are common on the Web: Word (.DOC) Acrobat (.PDF) and Postscript (.EPS or .PS).

Acrobat

PDF (Portable Document Format) is a cross-platform format devised by Adobe – the fonts and DTP people. A PDF file looks the same on a Windows or DOS PC, a Mac or a Unix machine – as long as a suitable reader is installed.

Get your copy from the Web at:

　　http://www.adobe.com

Look for the Acrobat Reader for Window and download *acroread.exe*. Run this to extract the files and install them into an Acrobat directory in one operation.

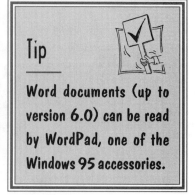

Tip
___

Word documents (up to version 6.0) can be read by WordPad, one of the Windows 95 accessories.

PDF files are compact. This 7 page document, with 3 illustrations, was 127Kb.

Ghostview & Ghostscript

GhostScript can read PostScript files and convert them for screen display – and for output to other printers. Ghostview, its companion program, is a graphical interface to Ghostscript – making it far simpler to use.

Download the software from Ghostview's home page:

http://www.cs.wisc.edu/~ghost/index.html

You will need these ZIPped files – about 3Mb in total.

gsview14.zip	Ghostview for Windows
gs353w32.zip	32-bit routines
gs353ini.zip	the core Ghostscript routines
gs353fn1.zip	PostScript fonts

There is a setup program in the 'gsview' file, plus detailed instructions in case the automatic installation doesn't work properly!

This illustration was created by opening the sample 'tiger.ps' file in Ghostview, grabbing the screenshot and importing it as a bitmap into this page. The page was then output as a PostScript file, and read back into Ghostview. Its screen was then grabbed again and reimported into the page!

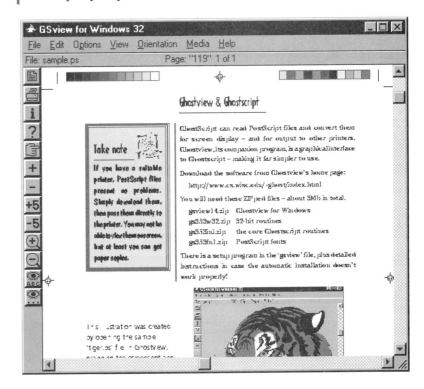

MSN Home page

Unless you change the Start page (see page 113), Internet
Explorer will start by going to the MSN home page. It's not
a bad place to start. From there you can step into a good
tutorial for "newbies", search the major catalogues or
browse through an excellent set of links – and, of course,
get lots of information about MSN and Microsoft's
products!

Basic steps

1 Go to MSN's home
page at:

http://www.msn.com

2 Click on **Customize
This Page**.

3 Set your options.

① Go to MSN   ② Click Customize

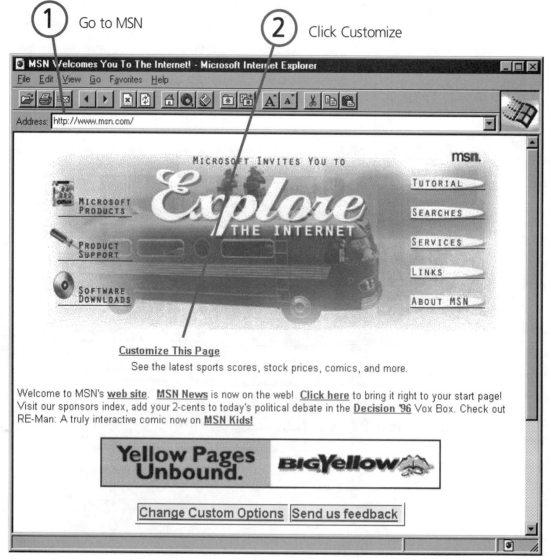

Customising the MSN Start page

4 Click `Set Up Page` to mail the options to MSN.

5 Make MSN your Start page for Explorer.

❑ Next time you connect, you will have your own personal start page.

An intriguing feature of the MSN home page is that you can customise it with your own links and selection of services, as well as colours and graphics styles. This is not restricted to MSN members, or to Explorer users.

Take note

The personalised start page is not a "home page". MSN does not (yet) offer home pages to its members.

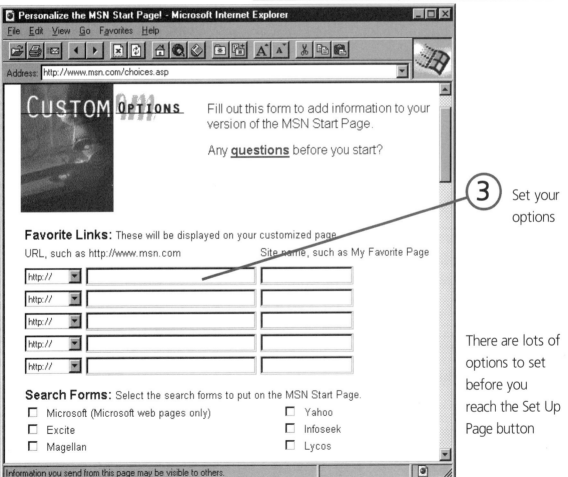

Favorite Links: These will be displayed on your customized page

Fill out this form to add information to your version of the MSN Start Page.

Any **questions** before you start?

③ Set your options

There are lots of options to set before you reach the Set Up Page button

World Wide Web

Once you have found something of interest on a Web page, it is usually fairly easy to find more on that same topic by following up hypertext links. Most people will include on their page at least a few links to related pages.

But you have to find that first point of entry and the big problem here is the sheer quantity of information. There are over 20 million pages (and countless gigabytes of files) accessible through the Web. With this amount of material around, how do you find where to start? There are two main approaches directories and searches.

Net Directories

These carry links to pages, organised into a hierarchy of topics. Some of the best directories are:

- Yahoo (*www.yahoo.com*) – very comprehensive and well-organised, with good cross-referencing;

- Lycos (*www.lycos.com*) – claims to have links to over 90% of all Web pages, with Hot Lists of the 250 most popular (and possibly most useful) sites;

- Global Network Navigator (*gnn.com/gnn/ GNNhome.html*) – with the excellent Whole Internet Catalog and a set of 2,000 selected sites;

- Magellan (*www.mckinley.com*) has detailed reviews of over 30,000 sites, with a "Green light" system to show those suitable for family viewing, plus summary details of another half million.

- UK directory (*www.ukdirectory.com*) – links to 3,000+ UK commercial, educational and government sites.

Take note

Any estimates of size and number on the Internet are out of date by the time they are published on paper. The Web alone is reckoned to be growing at the rate of around 1 million new pages each month!

Tip

If you start from MSN's home page, try their LINKS. Though the set is not as comprehensive as those in any of the Net directories, it is well organised and points to some useful places from which to start browsing.

Yahoo is organised by topic and sub-topic. You will normally have to work through three of four levels of menus before you come to pages of links – but when you get there, the links are relevant, and focussed. When you find a useful menu, it can be added to your Favorites list to give you a simple jump direct to it.

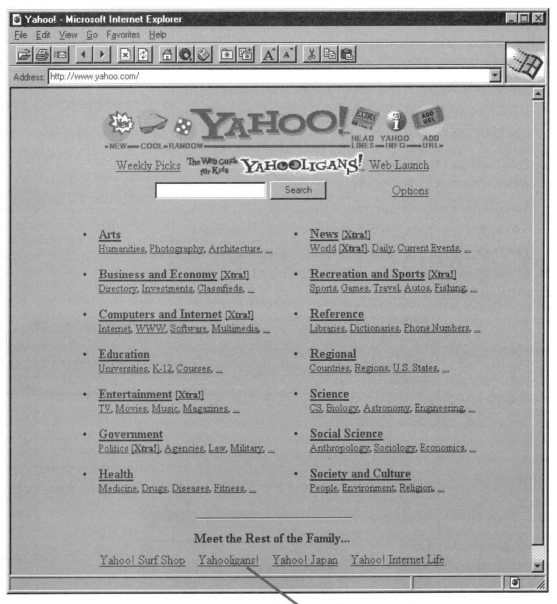

For kids, not surfing rowdies!

Searching the Web

The directories all offer search facilities, and you can reach the leading five from MSN's search page (see opposite.)

There are also other specialist search engines. Two of the best established of these are:

- WebCrawler (*webcrawler.com*) maintains a massive database of Web pages. Its searches are through both the title and contents of pages, and unless you give very specific search terms, you can get a lot of irrelevant hits.

- Open Text (*www.opentext.com*) claims to have indexed everything on the World Wide Web! A simple search here can also produce thousands of results. To get a shorter, more closely matched, set of pages, you can refine your search, or perform a "Power Search", using up to 5 words, linked by *And*, *Or* and other operators.

- ❏ Try you can find a single word that specifies what you are looking for. If you enter two, some search engines look for pages that include *both* words, others look for those that have *either*.

- ❏ If the initial search produces too many hits, you can usually redefine the search at the engine's site.

This will find pages that have all three words "graphics", "Conversion" and "windows" anywhere within the page.

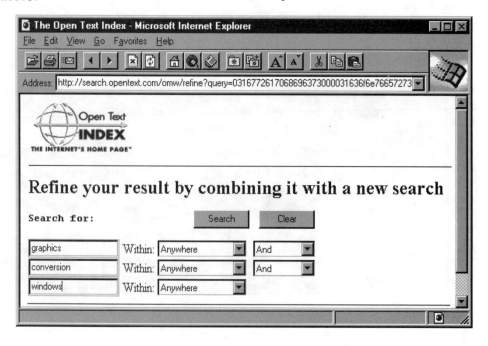

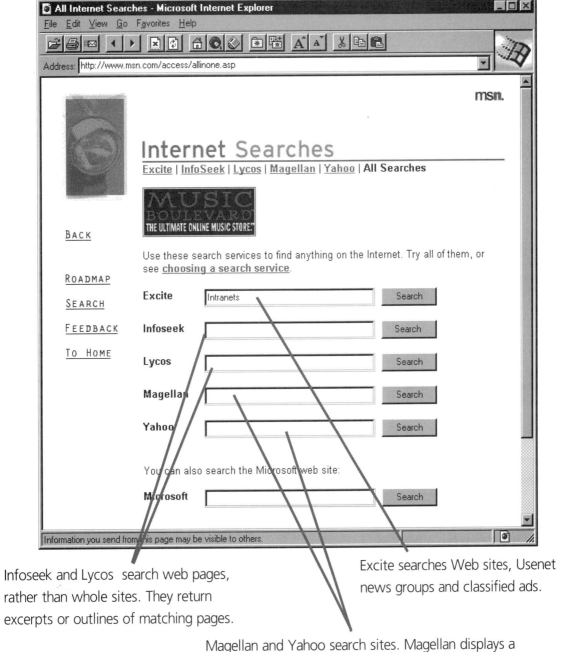

All Internet Searches - Microsoft Internet Explorer

File Edit View Go Favorites Help

Address: http://www.msn.com/access/allinone.asp

msn.

Internet Searches

Excite | InfoSeek | Lycos | Magellan | Yahoo | All Searches

MUSIC BOULEVARD
THE ULTIMATE ONLINE MUSIC STORE.™

BACK

ROADMAP

SEARCH

FEEDBACK

TO HOME

Use these search services to find anything on the Internet. Try all of them, or see **choosing a search service**.

Excite   Intranets   [Search]

Infoseek   [Search]

Lycos   [Search]

Magellan   [Search]

Yahoo   [Search]

You can also search the Microsoft web site:

Microsoft   [Search]

Information you send from this page may be visible to others.

Infoseek and Lycos search web pages, rather than whole sites. They return excerpts or outlines of matching pages.

Excite searches Web sites, Usenet news groups and classified ads.

Magellan and Yahoo search sites. Magellan displays a review and star-rating of matching sites. Yahoo also gives you links to the site's category in its directory.

125

Newsgroups

Explorer has built-in routines for handling newsgroups, and for finding and reading their articles.

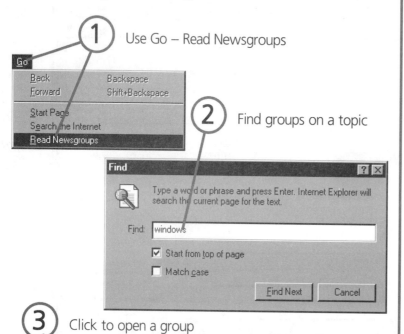

Use Go – Read Newsgroups

Find groups on a topic

Click to open a group

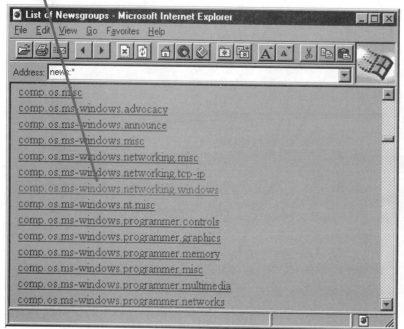

1 Open the **Go** menu and select **Read Newsgroups**.

❑ The first time you do this, there is a delay while the list of groups is downloaded.

2 Scroll through the (long!!) list, or use **Edit – Find** to track down groups on a topic.

3 Select a group.

4 Scroll through the list of articles and click to select one for reading.

5 From the reader screen you can post a reply or move to other articles.

Take note

If you can use MSN's news server, it bundles related groups into folders – each dot in the name marks a new level of folder. This is a much neater way of dealing with the groups.

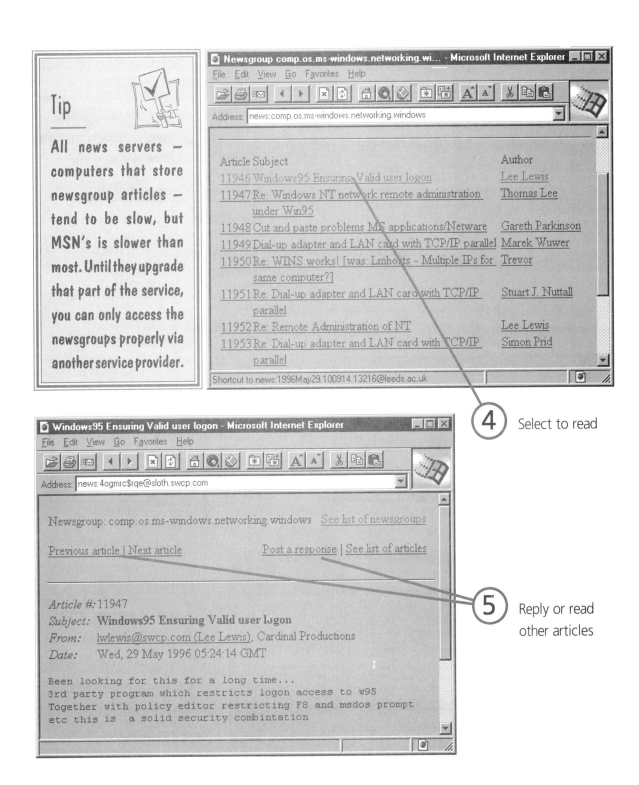

Newsgroup comp.os.ms-windows.networking.wi... - Microsoft Internet Explorer

File   Edit   View   Go   Favorites   Help

Address: news:comp.os.ms-windows.networking.windows

Article Subject   Author
11946 Windows95 Ensuring Valid user logon   Lee Lewis
11947 Re: Windows NT network remote administration   Thomas Lee
        under Win95
11948 Cut and paste problems MS applications/Netware   Gareth Parkinson
11949 Dial-up adapter and LAN card with TCP/IP parallel   Marek Wuwer
11950 Re: WINS works! [was: Lmhosts - Multiple IPs for   Trevor
        same computer?]
11951 Re: Dial-up adapter and LAN card with TCP/IP   Stuart J. Nuttall
        parallel
11952 Re: Remote Administration of NT   Lee Lewis
11953 Re: Dial-up adapter and LAN card with TCP/IP   Simon Prid
        parallel

Shortcut to news:1996May29.100914.13216@leeds.ac.uk

④ Select to read

Windows95 Ensuring Valid user logon - Microsoft Internet Explorer

File   Edit   View   Go   Favorites   Help

Address: news:4ogmrc$rqe@sloth.swcp.com

Newsgroup: comp.os.ms-windows.networking.windows   See list of newsgroups

Previous article | Next article   Post a response | See list of articles

_____

Article #: 11947
Subject: **Windows95 Ensuring Valid user logon**
From: lwlewis@swcp.com (Lee Lewis), Cardinal Productions
Date: Wed, 29 May 1996 05:24:14 GMT

Been looking for this for a long time...
3rd party program which restricts logon access to w95
Together with policy editor restricting F8 and msdos prompt
etc this is a solid security combintation

⑤ Reply or read
other articles

Intranets

The World Wide Web has proved to be such a powerful means of sharing ideas and files, that companies are now beginning to apply its approach to their internal communications. You cannot set up a fully-functioning Intranet without special Web server software – Explorer is only designed to handle the user's end of a Web link. However, there is enough in Explorer for you to be able to run a limited company-wide Web.

If you store the page(s) and their linked files in one shared folder, it is simple to create links between them. As linked files can be read, viewed or downloaded by anyone on the nextwork, the page can be used to circulate news, templates and other common files throughout the company.

Basic steps

❑ **Opening a home page**

1 In Explorer, use **File – Open** or click 📂 to open the **Open Internet Address** dialog box

2 Click [Open File...]

3 Work up and over the network to find the main page.

4 Use **Favorites – Add to Favorites** to store the address.

❑ Next time you want to open the page, you just click on it in the **Favorites** list.

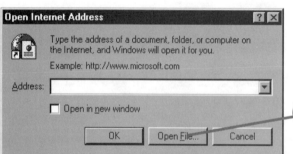

② Click Open File

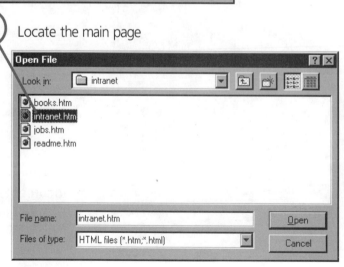

③ Locate the main page

Tip

World Wide Web – and intranet – pages are written using HTML (HyperText Markup Language). See "Designing Internet Home Pages Made Simple" for more on this.

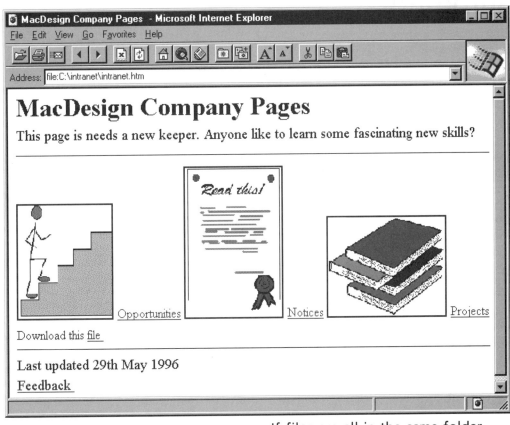

```
<HTML>
<HEAD>
<TITLE>
MacDesign Company Pages
</TITLE>
</HEAD>
<BODY>
<BODY BACKGROUND = "mac1.gif" BGCOLOR = "#ffffff" TEXT = "#00000f0">
<H1>MacDesign Company Pages</H2>
<FONT SIZE = 4>
This page is needs a new keeper. Anyone like to learn some fascinating new skills?
<HR>
<FONT size = 3>
<A HREF = author.htm><IMG  Align=Bottom SRC="jobs.gif">Opportunities</A>
<A HREF = readme.htm><IMG  Align=Bottom SRC="readme.gif">Notices</A>
<A HREF = books.htm><IMG  Align=Bottom SRC="books.gif">Projects</A>
<P>Download this <A HREF = prelims.doc> file </A>
<HR>
</FONT>
Last updated 29th May 1996 <p>
<A HREF = feedback.htm> Feedback </A>
</BODY>
</HTML>
```

If files are all in the same folder, you only need their filenames in the link. If they are elsewhere, you will have to work out the path.

You can link to graphics, other pages, and to documents and other files for downloading

Summary

- ❏ The Internet links many millions of computers world-wide and gives access to huge quantities of data.

- ❏ Internet Explorer is one of the leading Web browsers and a natural choice for MSN users.

- ❏ You can set options to customise the Explorer display and ways of working.

- ❏ Viewers can be set as registered file types to enable Explorer to handle a greater variety of files.

- ❏ Lview Pro is a compact and efficient viewer/editor that can handle the main graphic formats.

- ❏ Paint Shop Pro is probably the most comprehensive graphics shareware package available at present.

- ❏ Though most text is plain ASCII, some documents are formatted.

- ❏ The Acrobat Reader is needed to viewer PDF files.

- ❏ Ghostview and Ghostscript are needed to display and print For PostScript files.

- ❏ The MSN Home page is a good place to start surfing the Net. You can customise it to include your own selection of links and information.

- ❏ The World Wide Web offers a simple and attractive way of reaching almost all parts of the Internet.

- ❏ There are directories and search engines to help you find information on the Web

- ❏ There are newsgroups on virtually every topic.

- ❏ You can create a simple intranets on your own LAN, using Explorer.

9 Microsoft fax

Setting up

Every machine that will be used for sending or receiving faxes must have the Microsoft Fax software installed, and the Properties properly configured.

Start with the computer that hosts the modem.

After you run the Add/Remove Programs to install the software, your Start menu will contain a new group – Fax.

The first time that you use any one of these programs, a Wizard will run to link the fax into the Exchange system.

Run a Fax program

● Run this first on the computer that hosts the modem, and share the fax onto the network before setting up the other computers.

Set up the connected modem first

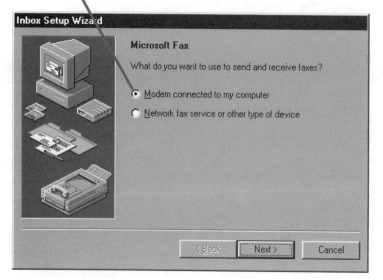

Basic steps

1 Click **Start**, and select **Programs – Accessories – Fax** then **Compose New Fax**.

2 At the first panel, select **connected** or **Network** modem, to suit the machine.

3 Next select the **modem**, if more than one is available.

4 If you want to receive incoming faxes, tick **Yes** and set the number of **rings**.

5 Enter your **Name** and **Fax number**, as you want them to appear on the faxes you send.

6 You can set Exchange to run on startup, if required.

Take note

A fax behaves like a printer. Any application that can print can also send faxes.

(4) Answer incoming calls?

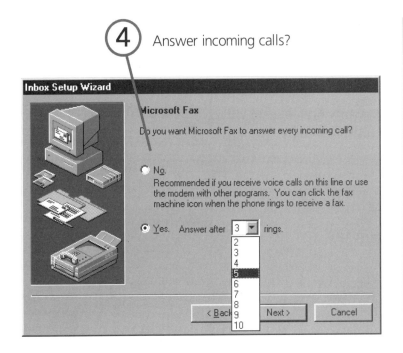

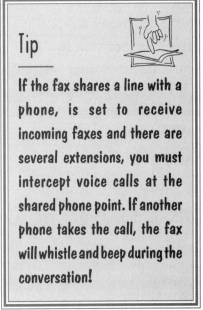

Tip

If the fax shares a line with a phone, is set to receive incoming faxes and there are several extensions, you must intercept voice calls at the shared phone point. If another phone takes the call, the fax will whistle and beep during the conversation!

If auto-answering, how long do you need to intercept incoming voice calls?

Take note

After it has done its work, the Wizard will take you on into the selected program. Stop it at that point, and set the Fax's Exchange properties before using it in earnest.

(5) Identification for outgoing faxes

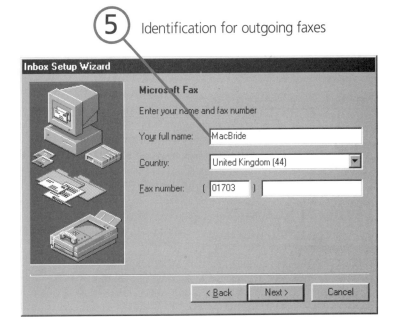

Fax on the network

When you share a fax across the network, the access is not to the hardware itself, but to a folder in which faxes are stored as they wait to go out, or as they come in down the line. The new folder (called 'Netfax') and the fax's link to it are set up automatically, but the system doesn't tell you that it has done this. You have to find the network path to that folder if you want to connect other computers to it.

Basic steps

❑ Sharing the fax

1 Right click Inbox on the Desktop and select **Properties**.

2 Select **Microsoft Fax** and click Properties

3 Go to the **Modem** tab.

4 Tick the **Share...** box.

Leave the Modem Properties at the defaults for now

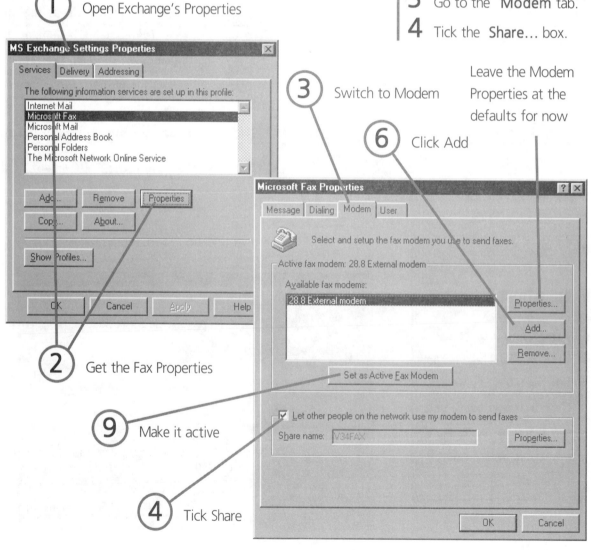

(1) Open Exchange's Properties

(3) Switch to Modem

(6) Click Add

(2) Get the Fax Properties

(9) Make it active

(4) Tick Share

5 Run **My Computer** to find the Netfax folder, and work out its Network path.

❏ **Making the link**

Move to a networked computer and take steps 1 to 3 there.

6 Click [Add...]

7 At the **Add a Fax Modem** dialog, select **Network fax server**.

8 Enter the network path to the Netfax folder.

9 Select the fax and click [Set as Active Fax Modem]

Take note

Network paths are covered on page 74.

What's the network name of this computer?

⑤ Find the folder

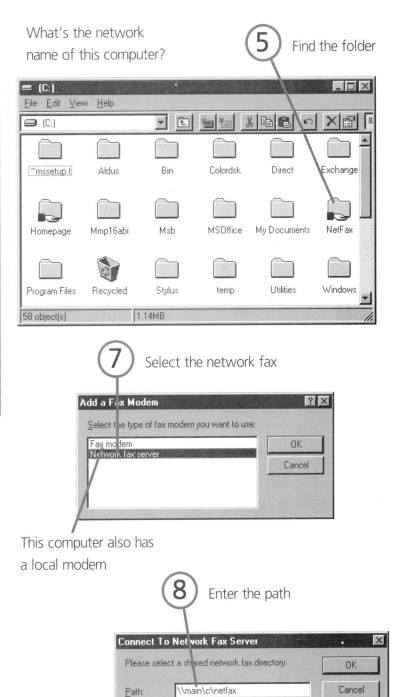

⑦ Select the network fax

This computer also has a local modem

⑧ Enter the path

Cover pages

Cover page can be very useful. They identify who sent the fax and who it is sent to – essential where one fax serves a whole office. If you want to send a brief note, it can be written within the Compose Wizard and embedded in the page. If you are sending a document created in Word or other application, it can be attached easily to a cover page.

There are four ready made cover pages, and an editor in which you can customize them or create your own.

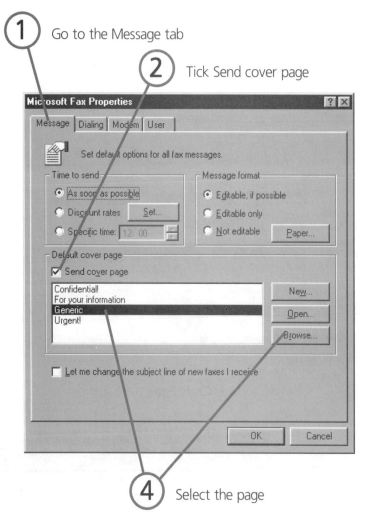

(1) Go to the Message tab

(2) Tick Send cover page

(4) Select the page

1 Open the **Microsoft Fax Properties** panel at the **Message** tab.

2 Tick the **Send cover page** box.

3 Select a default page from the list, or **Browse** for one you have created – the file will have a .CPE extension.

❑ **Editing a cover page**

4 Click 🔲 **Start** and select **Programs – Accessories – Fax – Cover Page Editor**.

5 Open an existing file for editing – they are in the Windows/System folder – or create your own from scratch.

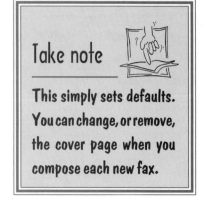

Take note
─────────
This simply sets defaults. You can change, or remove, the cover page when you compose each new fax.

⑤ Open a file in the Cover Page Editor

Sender and Recipient details and other items in {brackets} will be drawn from your settings and from information entered when composing the fax. To add another of these to a fax, select it from the Insert menu and drag a box to show where it should fit.

You can set the font, size and styles of selected fields.

Add new text

Add boxes, lines or other graphics

Click on a field to select it – hold [Ctrl] and click to select a set.

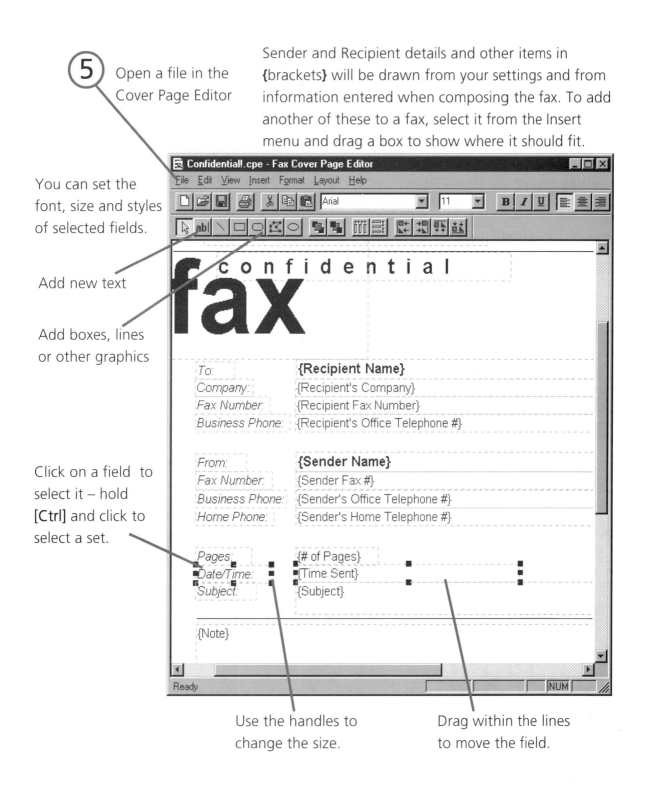

Confidential!.cpe - Fax Cover Page Editor

File Edit View Insert Format Layout Help

Arial   11   **B** *I* <u>U</u>

confidential
fax

To:	{Recipient Name}
Company:	{Recipient's Company}
Fax Number:	{Recipient Fax Number}
Business Phone:	{Recipient's Office Telephone #}

From:	{Sender Name}
Fax Number:	{Sender Fax #}
Business Phone:	{Sender's Office Telephone #}
Home Phone:	{Sender's Home Telephone #}

Pages:	{# of Pages}
Date/Time:	{Time Sent}
Subject:	{Subject}

{Note}

Ready   NUM

Use the handles to change the size.

Drag within the lines to move the field.

137

Sending a fax

You can send faxes from any application with File – Print, selecting the fax as the printer, but the simplest approach is to use the Compose Wizard. It takes you through the stages, collecting the data as it goes. If your message is brief, write it as a note within the Wizard. A long message is better written in a word processor, saved as a file and attached to a cover page.

1 Click **Start** and select **Programs – Accessories – Fax – Compose New Fax**.

2 The first time you send a fax, you will be asked where you are dialling from. If you always fax from the same place, tick the check box.

3 Click **Address Book..**

4 Open your Personal Address Book – fax numbers are held there.

① Run the Compose Wizard

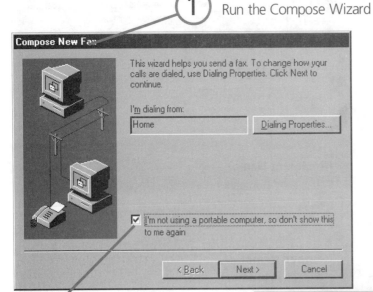

② Check if on a fixed system

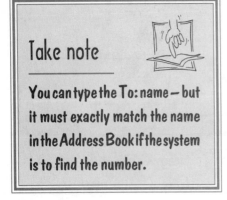

Take note

You can type the To: name – but it must exactly match the name in the Address Book if the system is to find the number.

③ Click Address Book

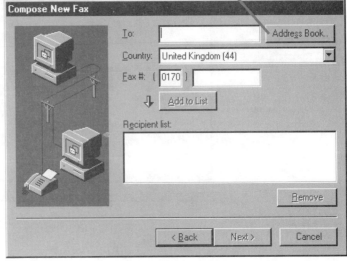

5 Select the recipient(s) and click ⟦ To -> ⟧

6 At the next panel, select a cover page.

7 Click ⟦ Options... ⟧ if you want to set the **Time to send** or the **Message format**.

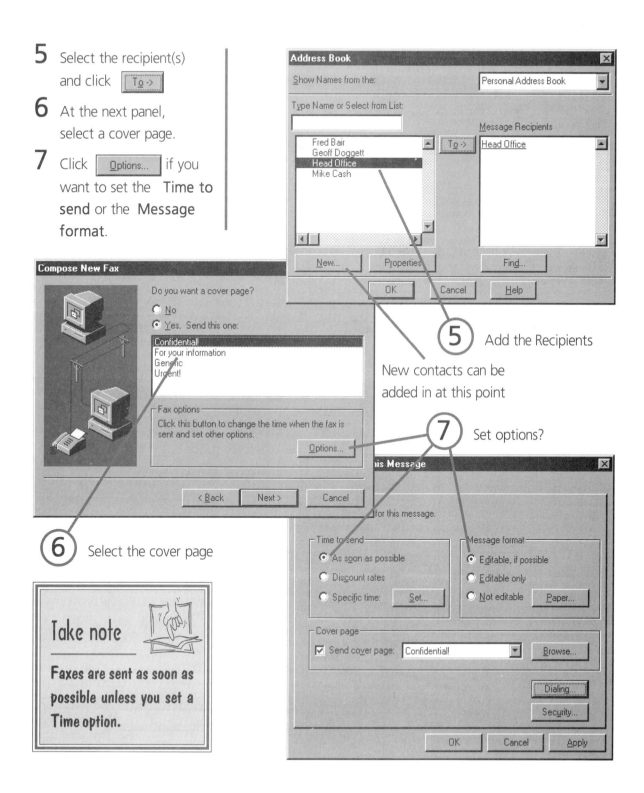

Address Book

Show Names from the: Personal Address Book ▼

Type Name or Select from List:

[   ]   Message Recipients

Fred Bair   ▲   ⟦ To -> ⟧   Head Office   ▲
Geoff Doggett
Head Office
Mike Cash
                   ▼   ▼

⟦ New... ⟧   ⟦ Properties ⟧   ⟦ Find... ⟧

⟦ OK ⟧   ⟦ Cancel ⟧   ⟦ Help ⟧

⑤ Add the Recipients

New contacts can be added in at this point

⑦ Set options?

Compose New Fax

Do you want a cover page?

○ No
◉ Yes. Send this one:

Confidential!
For your information
Generic
Urgent!

┌ Fax options ─────────────────────────┐
│ Click this button to change the time when the fax is │
│ sent and set other options.   │
│   ⟦ Options... ⟧   │
└──────────────────────────────────────┘

⟦ < Back ⟧   ⟦ Next > ⟧   ⟦ Cancel ⟧

⑥ Select the cover page

...is Message

...for this message.

┌ Time to send ──────────┐   ┌ Message format ──────────┐
│ ◉ As soon as possible   │   │ ◉ Editable, if possible   │
│ ○ Discount rates   │   │ ○ Editable only   │
│ ○ Specific time: ⟦ Set... ⟧ │   │ ○ Not editable ⟦ Paper... ⟧ │
└─────────────────────────┘   └───────────────────────────┘

┌ Cover page ──┐
│ ☑ Send cover page: Confidential! ▼   ⟦ Browse... ⟧ │
└───┘

                                         ⟦ Dialing... ⟧
                                         ⟦ Security... ⟧

⟦ OK ⟧   ⟦ Cancel ⟧   ⟦ Apply ⟧

Take note

Faxes are sent as soon as possible unless you set a Time option.

139

Basic steps

8 Type the Subject

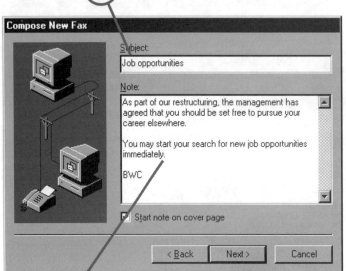

9 Use the Note for a brief message

8 Type in a **Subject** – this will be shown on the cover page and in the recipient's Inbox list.

9 For short messages, just type a **Note** for the cover page.

10 To send a pre-written file, click [Add File...] and browse your folders to locate it.

Tip

Faxes are sent as graphics, so you can attach pictures or other files containing images.

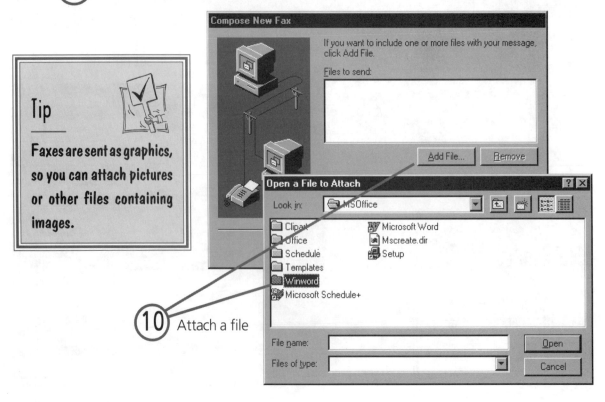

10 Attach a file

Basic steps

1 Open the **Microsoft Fax Properties** panel at the **Modem** tab, as shown on page 134.

2 Click [Properties]

3 Select **Manual** if the phone line is also used for voice calls.

or

4 Select **Answer after**, and set the number of **rings**, if only faxes are expected on that line.

5 Click [OK]

You can switch modes at any time – the new setting comes into effect immediately.

Receiving faxes

If you want to receive faxes through your system, you must set the modem to answer the phone – either automatically or after you have had a check for a voice first.

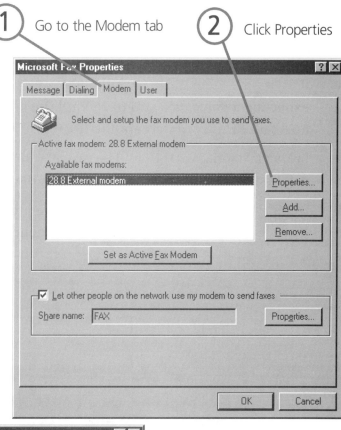

① Go to the Modem tab

② Click Properties

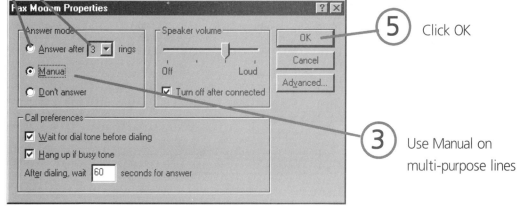

④ Use auto-answer on dedicated lines

⑤ Click OK

③ Use Manual on multi-purpose lines

Incoming faxes

When the fax is set to answer, it will swing into action when an incoming call is detected.

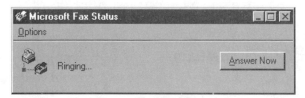

- If it is in automatic answer mode and you are expecting a voice call, you have until the specified number of rings to intercept the fax.

- In Manual mode, use the handset to check for a voice call first, before setting the fax loose on the line.

- Don't replace the handset until you have picked up the call with the fax, or you will break the connection.

The new fax will be stored in your Inbox.

Take note

When a fax is received successfully, you will get a new mail message, and the icon will appear on the status bar.

Faxes can be recognised by their special icon

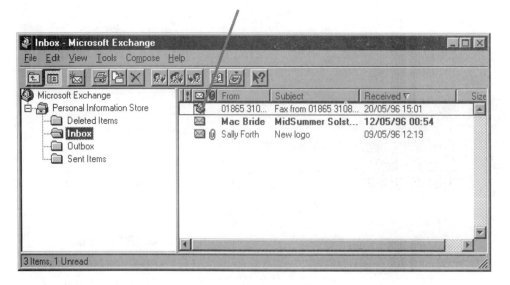

Basic steps

1 Double click the fax item in Exchange to open it in **Fax Viewer**.

2 Use ⟲⟳ to rotate the image if needed.

3 Use the ⊕⊖ to zoom in and out.

4 Click 🖨 for a printout.

Reading and printing

When you open the fax to read it, Exchange runs Fax Viewer. This includes tools for zooming in (and out), and for rotating – very handy if you have been sent a sideways on drawing.

With these facilities for examining the fax, you may not need a paper copy. If you do want one, Fax Viewerwill give you a good quality, long-lasting printout – better than most dedicated fax machines.

Select mode – selected parts can be copied into Paint, Word or other applications

Drag mode (slides fax around in the window)

Thumbnails on/off

Set Zoom level

③ Zoom

② Rotate?

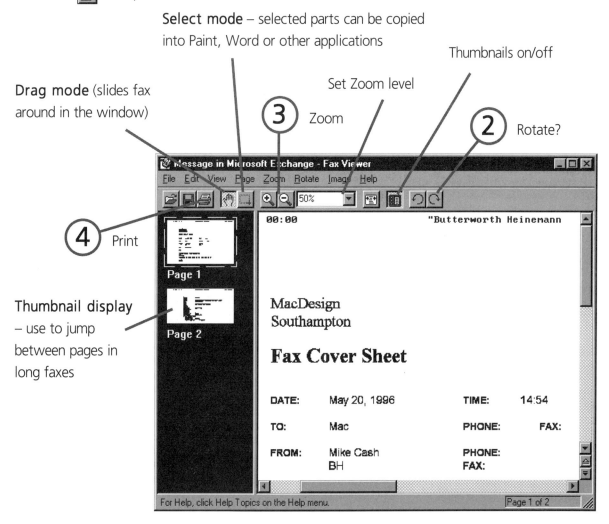

④ Print

Thumbnail display – use to jump between pages in long faxes

Summary

❑ For fax communications there must be a suitable modem attached to your computer or one shared over the network.

❑ If the fax shares the line with the voice phone, it is best kept under manual control.

❑ Microsoft Fax must be installed on every machine that is to send or receive faxes.

❑ The fax is configured and used very like a printer.

❑ When using a fax over the network, it is not the machine, but the Netfax folder that must be shared.

❑ Cover pages can be sent if required. You can edit existing cover pages or create your own with the special editor.

❑ The Compose Wizard offers the simplest way to send a fax. The message can either be written within the Wizard or attached as a file.

❑ Faxes are received and read through Exchange, using the special Fax Viewer.

Index

146

The Internet for Windows 3.1 Made Simple   ISBN 07506 2311 X

The Internet for Windows 95 Made Simple   ISBN 07506 2835 9

All you need to get you started.

If you want to know how to:

❑ **set up hardware and software to get on-line**

❑ **find the best service provider for your needs**

❑ **send e-mail, read the news and download files from around the world**

❑ **explore the World Wide Web**

then one of these **Made Simples** is for you !

By a combination of **tutorial approach**, with **tasks to do** and **easy steps**, the **Made Simple** series of Computer Books stands above all others.

Readers comments on The Internet for Windows 3.1 Made Simple include:

● 'An excellent book. Congratulations to the Author.'

● 'It's not that often that I find a computer book that has been informative as well as enjoyable to read. Your book has enabled me to understand the Internet at least to a level that I can start to explore without fear.'

● 'After buying what seemed like a hundred books on Internet access I eventually acquired your "*Internet Made Simple*" and found it far more helpful than anything else I had previously waded through. I have everything up and running well and feel quite pleased I've survived the steep learning curve. Thank you.'

● 'Thankyou for saving my sanity with your excellent, clear, concise book on the Internet. I browsed through dozens of books, none of which seemed right, before choosing yours. Nice to read something so clear, up-to-date, focused on the kind of software I was using and not biased towards the US !!'

Available from all good bookshops, or in case of difficulty, contact:
Heinemann Publishers, Oxford, P.O.Box 381,Oxford OX2 8EJ.
Tel 01865 314300. Fax 01865 314091. Credit card sales 01865 314627.

8 – 17
22 – 25
57 – 59